Bridging
the
Values Gap

How Authentic Organizations
Bring Values to Life

R. Edward Freeman   Ellen R. Auster

Berrett–Koehler Publishers, Inc.
a BK Business book

Berrett-Koehler Publishers, Inc.
1333 Broadway, Suite 1000, Oakland, CA 94612-1921
Tel: (510) 817-2277   Fax: (510) 817-2278   www.bkconnection.com

Ordering Information

Quantity sales. Special discounts are available on quantity purchases by corporations, associations, and others. For details, contact the "Special Sales Department" at the Berrett-Koehler address above.

Individual sales. Berrett-Koehler publications are available through most bookstores. They can also be ordered directly from Berrett-Koehler:

Tel: (800) 929-2929; Fax: (802) 864-7626; www.bkconnection.com.

Orders for college textbook/course adoption use. Please contact Berrett-Koehler:

Tel: (800) 929-2929; Fax: (802) 864-7626.

Orders by U.S. trade bookstores and wholesalers. Please contact Ingram Publisher Services, Tel: (800) 509-4887; Fax: (800) 838-1149; E-mail: customer.service@ ingrampublisherservices.com; or visit www.ingrampublisherservices.com/Ordering for details about electronic ordering.

Berrett-Koehler and the BK logo are registered trademarks of Berrett-Koehler Publishers, Inc.

Printed in the United States of America

Berrett-Koehler books are printed on long-lasting acid-free paper. When it is available, we choose paper that has been manufactured by environmentally responsible processes. These may include using trees grown in sustainable forests, incorporating recycled paper, minimizing chlorine in bleaching, or recycling the energy produced at the paper mill.

Library of Congress Cataloging-in-Publication Data
Freeman, R. Edward, 1951–
  Bridging the values gap : how authentic organizations bring values to life / R. Edward Freeman and Ellen R. Auster. — First Edition.
      pages cm
  Includes bibliographical references and index.
  ISBN 978-1-60994-956-3 (hardcover)
1. Value. 2. Economic value added. 3. Strategic planning—Employee participation.
I. Auster, Ellen R. II. Title.
  HG223.F74 2015
  658.4'08—dc23
                                                              2015011063

19   18   17   16   15   10   9   8   7   6   5   4   3   2   1

Cover design by Richard Adelson. Cover illustration © Caiaimage.
Interior design and composition by Gary Palmatier, Ideas to Images. Elizabeth von Radics, copyeditor; Mike Mollett, proofreader; Rachel Rice, indexer.

*To the memory of my grandmother Ruby Odom Andrews,
who inspired me to think about the issues in this book and
who taught me more about values than I can ever repay.*

—R. EDWARD FREEMAN

*To my parents, Don and Nancy Auster, for their
eternal love and support and for being brilliant role models
and nurturers of how to lead authentic, inspired,
connected, and reflective values-centered lives.*

—ELLEN R. AUSTER

Contents

Foreword   ix

Preface   xiii

PART **I**

Understanding the Values Gap in Business   1

   CHAPTER **1**

   The Values Gap in Business   3

   CHAPTER **2**

   Just Be Authentic: Not So Fast, Not So Easy   17

   CHAPTER **3**

   Authentic Organizations: Is Yours One?   31

   CHAPTER **4**

   Do Values Right or Don't Do Them at All   47

PART **II**

How Businesses Can Bridge the Values Gap   65

   CHAPTER **5**

   Introspective Values:
   Reflecting on Self and the Organization   67

CHAPTER **6**

Historical Values:
Exploring the Impact of Our Past   91

CHAPTER **7**

Connectedness Values:
Creating a Sense of Belonging and Community   111

CHAPTER **8**

Aspirational Values: Our Hopes and Dreams   137

PART **III**

Bringing the Conversation to Life   157

CHAPTER **9**

Getting Started   159

Notes   169

Index   181

About the Authors   191

Foreword

by John Mackey and Raj Sisodia

Ed Freeman and Ellen Auster have written the definitive guide to thinking about and implementing a values-based approach to business. They provide a wealth of compelling examples and offer very practical frameworks for companies to successfully navigate this rocky terrain.

As longtime proponents of conscious capitalism, we strongly believe that values are foundational for companies looking to embody a more conscious way of doing business. Values inform a company's purpose, which is one of the four key tenets of conscious capitalism, along with stakeholder integration, conscious leadership, and conscious culture. The collection of values that are core to a company compose its culture. The values of the company's leaders must be in harmony with the espoused values of the organization, which have to resonate with all stakeholders—so getting values right is essential to the practice of conscious capitalism. This book will go a long way in helping people think logically and comprehensively about values.

Shared values are a precursor to creating "shared value," which is another way that people are starting to think about the evolution of business. At Whole Foods Market, we think of our core values as the guiding principles that we can use to realize our purpose. Our core values are very real to us; we share them with all of our stakeholders and continuously are in dialogue about them. The core values are: selling the highest-quality natural and organic products available, satisfying and delighting our customers, supporting team member happiness and excellence, creating wealth through profits and growth, caring about our communities and the environment, creating ongoing win-win partnerships with our suppliers, and promoting the health of our stakeholders through healthy-eating education.

Core values are essential in helping leaders deal with dilemmas where they have to choose between multiple courses of action that each seems right from a certain perspective. In such cases, leaders can use a company's core values to make choices that are maximally beneficial to all stakeholders. Instead of simply choosing one approach over another, we strive to come up with a creative solution that can simultaneously fulfill multiple values.

For example, Whole Foods Market sells a full range of animal-based foods because 95 percent of our customers eat these foods. At the same time, we have a commitment to improving the health and longevity of our customers and to improving animal welfare. We need to reconcile satisfying and delighting our customers while also helping them be as healthy as possible. Research shows that reducing the consumption of animal-based foods is a key aspect of improving health. Our approach is to educate our customers about the benefits of eating minimally processed and unrefined plant foods while also working to provide them with the healthiest possible animal-based products and ensuring that those animals are humanely treated. This approach has allowed us to remain true to our values while also remaining viable as a business.

The real test of a company's commitment to its stated values comes when it faces an existential threat. If a company can hold steady and not sacrifice its core values under such conditions, it augurs well for its ability to thrive in the long run. For example, Southwest Airlines—a highly conscious business—has famously stayed loyal to its employees through numerous downturns in the airline market; it has never laid off any employees in its history.

During the great recession of 2008–2009, many companies faced extremely tough conditions and had to make difficult decisions. Truly conscious companies rededicate themselves to their core values in such times, enabling them to survive with their culture strengthened and their humanity intact. One example is a company called Barry-Wehmiller, a $2 billion privately held industrial machinery manufacturer based in St. Louis, Missouri. When the downturn hit, new orders for capital equipment virtually dried up. The company hoped it could get by on its backlog of orders as well as its aftermarket parts and services business. Soon, however, customers started to cancel existing orders, walking away from multimillion-dollar commitments. The situation was dire, and the board of directors was recommending that the company start looking at layoffs. CEO Bob Chapman, however, was guided by the opening line in the company's vision and values document, called its Guiding Principles of Leadership: *We measure success by the way we touch the lives of people.*

This document was deeply meaningful to everyone in the company and had been a touchstone for decision making since it was formulated six years earlier. Every major decision was looked at through the lens of the impact that it would have on all the lives that the company touched. As Chapman thought about the consequences of laying off a significant proportion of his workforce, he decided that he simply could not do that and remain true to the company's highest values. In that economic environment, there were simply no manufacturing jobs to be had. Numerous families would lose their homes, their children would have to be pulled out of college, and marriages might crumble. Bob thought, *How would a caring family respond to this kind of crisis?* The answer came to him: the family would pull together, and everyone would make sacrifices so that no one family member had to suffer excessively.

He came up with the creative idea of instituting a furlough: everyone in the company would take an average of one month off without pay. The company froze contributions to the 401(k) plan, lowered some executive salaries, and cut back on expenses such as travel. This enabled the company to save enough money to stay in compliance with its banking covenants and ensure that no layoffs were needed. The action resulted in an outpouring of goodwill, even altruism; some employees offered to take additional time off so that their colleagues who could not afford to take a month off could take less. By the time the recession ended, the culture had been strengthened and morale was higher than ever. The company's business recovered far ahead of the industry, and it gained significant market share, as it had experienced staff ready to work while other firms were scrambling to rehire people.

One of the powerful tools that is presented in this book is the idea of values through conversation. Barry-Wehmiller uses a version of this approach that it refers to as "mind the gap." After a team of people from across the company had drafted the Guiding Principles of Leadership, leaders across the organization sat down with small groups and shared the document with them. The leaders said, "These are the values that we say we live by. Please tell us where we are falling short." This resulted in numerous instances in which team members pointed out policies and practices that were inconsistent with the Guiding Principles of Leadership. The company immediately changed each of those policies. Over time such gaps virtually disappeared, and the company now has a remarkable level of consistency in being true to all of its stated values.

The values that a company chooses to live by can also be thought of as virtues. Just as all of us as individuals should strive to embody the essential human virtues, our organizations too should reflect them. But until now this has seemed an impossibly complex undertaking. This book helps resolve that complexity and enables organizations of any size to implement a values-centered approach to business. This in turn will spawn many more conscious businesses in the world, which will contribute greatly to human flourishing. We commend and thank Ed and Ellen for this valuable contribution.

Preface

M uch has been written about the role of values in business. There is, however, a real gap between the writings of business thinkers and pundits and what executives actually have the capability to do. Collectively, we have worked with organizations on values issues for more than 50 years, helping executives build the capability to understand and act on their values. Given the realities of the business world in the twenty-first century, we believe it is time for one more book—one that goes beyond platitudes and acknowledges how difficult it is to know and act on one's values consistently. Values are the wellspring—the foundation—of building a great company.

Business today is inarguably global. There are clashes of values and culture that go on continuously both inside and outside most companies, large and small. We believe that the idea that values are the most important component of how any business creates value is the most important insight in twenty-first-century capitalism as it is practiced around the globe. And there are many misunderstandings about how values work that lead to expensive mistakes. We need a more robust and realistic perspective about values in business, and this book provides such a view. We wrote this book to help executives think through how to be more effective in articulating and acting on their values both personally and in their business lives. We call this view *values through conversation (VTC)*.

What is a value? We will start the conversation here and elaborate in chapter 2. We take a very pragmatic view about values. They represent what is most important to us. Values necessitate a shared understanding of how we are going to behave. When we say that one of our values is *integrity,* it means that being honest with each other is very important to us. It also means that we need a common understanding, which is often a work in progress, about appropriate behaviors that bring that value to life. Of course, our own values can conflict with one another as well as with those of other people; and the business world constantly produces new situations that demand one think about the values that are appropriate. All of these reasons, and others, are important if we are to bridge the values gap in business.

Structure of the Book

The argument of the book works like this: In part I (chapters 1 through 4), we explain why many businesses have a values gap, and we give many examples from our experience. In part II (chapters 5 through 8), we focus on how to bridge these values gaps and suggest that creating a living conversation about a company's values is the key to success. In part III (chapter 9), we briefly summarize our conclusions and then explore three examples of values gaps and offer specific suggestions for next steps in bringing values to life.

The idea of "values" that has gained some currency in business in recent years is more complex than it first seems. Overall, we need to see acting on values as ongoing conversations in companies that shape options, choices, decisions, and actions as opposed to words that have been carved into stone or embossed on a "values card."

In chapter 1 we set out our view of the values gap that exists for many businesses. In chapter 2 we show how values work in our personal lives, leading to a lifelong project of self-discovery and creation; the chapter focuses on conversations that we have, often with ourselves, about who we are and who we can become. Chapter 3 looks at organizational values and the challenges associated with a business that wants to act on its values. Chapter 4 is a collection of mistakes that we have seen from our experience working with companies on these issues; we show how organizations limit their possibilities for growth and undermine their good intentions by making mistakes that could be avoided.

Chapters 5 through 8 give a detailed account of our method for bridging the values gap, with four different types of values through conversation. Each of these chapters starts with an At a Glance that captures the benefits, principles, and practices of how authentic organizations bring values to life through that form of VTC.

First, there is introspection, the subject of chapter 5. We cannot say much about our values if we are not willing to seriously probe and question our own motives and behavior. Second, there is our history, explored in chapter 6. We are at least partially products of our upbringing, our environment, and our experiences. Understanding different views of our history helps us figure out how to refresh and reinvent what we do while preserving legacy and continuity. Third, we are connected to others, as discussed in chapter 7, which explores and offers insights from companies on how to bridge the values gap through relationships with stakeholders and how to interact, lead, follow, and work together. Finally, we have aspirations—things we want to accomplish, ways we want to live, and our hopes, dreams, and fears—the subject of chapter 8.

Our argument is that by understanding introspective, historical, connectedness, and aspirational aspects of our values, we can bring values to life in our organizations through our conversations; this leads to decisions and actions that bridge the gap between the "talk" and the "walk." And, we argue, if these conversations are authentic, the possibilities for that organization are unlimited. We close with chapter 9, where we summarize our approach and point the way forward.

Method and Sources

Throughout this book we have relied on a number of sources. The first and most important is the broad group of business leaders whom we have had the privilege to work with over the past 25 years. To protect their anonymity, we often refer to them and their companies in a generic manner, such as "Mark was an executive in a multinational corporation." Such examples come from our personal observations and experience. When you see an actual company name, we have either a published source or permission from the company to use that example. Please note that all of our examples are real, and they represent our interpretations of the 50-plus years of our experience helping companies and executives, as well as our own interpretations of the business press, case studies, and other business writing. We are grateful for the experiences and conversations that have so profoundly shaped our thinking.

A second group of businesspeople who have molded our thinking is our students. Both of us teach seasoned executives with many years of experience and wisdom, as well as MBA students with just a few years of experience and a millennial point of view. We have learned a great deal from our students, and we hope that they will recognize some of the ideas, stories, and material in this book as emerging from the discussions and conversations in our classes.

A third set of sources we have benefitted from greatly comprises colleagues around the world, who have spent their careers trying to understand how values in business really work. These thought leaders are consultants, academics, and executives who will recognize what we have learned from them and see their influence on our thinking.

Acknowledgments

The ideas in this book were originally developed in two academic articles, as well as many other things we have written over the course of our careers. These are the main influences on this book: Ellen R.

Auster and R. Edward Freeman, "Values and Poetic Organizations: Beyond Value Fit toward Values through Conversation," *Journal of Business Ethics* 113, no. 1 (2013): 39–49, doi: 10.1007/s10551-012-1279-5; and R. Edward Freeman and Ellen R. Auster, "Values, Authenticity, and Responsible Leadership," *Journal of Business Ethics* 98, no. 1 (suppl.) (2011): 15–23, doi: 10.1007/s10551-011-1022-7. We are grateful to publishers and editors for giving us permission to recast and reuse this material.

In addition, we would like to express our personal thanks to a number of people and organizations that have supported us and helped us in the process of writing this book.

We are indebted to the team at Berrett-Koehler (BK). Special thanks and gratitude to Neal Maillet, our editor, for inviting us to have the conversation that started this book after he saw us speak at a conscious capitalism conference in Boston and for his deft but calm handling of the publishing process from start to finish. From crowdsourcing the title to suggestions during our Author Day visit, Neal and the BK team improved this book in so many ways. Thank you to Dianne Platner for her patience and openness with the cover design process. Gary Palmatier handled the production and internal design superbly, and Elizabeth von Radics was phenomenal with the final edit. Steve Piersanti has been a beacon for us throughout the history of Berrett-Koehler as a values-driven organization. His support for our work here has been invaluable.

In addition, we each would like to thank those in our personal circles of support.

Ed Freeman

I would like to thank the Darden School at the University of Virginia, and its sponsor trustees, as well as the Olsson Center for Applied Ethics, the Business Roundtable Institute for Corporate Ethics, and the Institute for Business in Society—all of which have generously supported work on this book. Lauren Purnell, Sergiy Dmytriyev, and the entire ethics team at Darden have made this book better. Conversations with Jim Freeland, Jared Harris, Bidhan Parmar, Sankaran Venkataraman, Andrew Wicks, and others have enriched our understanding of what it means to be authentic and act on one's values. Jenny Mead has made this a much more readable book. And without the daily support of Karen Musselman, the book simply would not exist.

Ellen Auster

Thank you to the Schulich School of Business for their financial support of this work. Bori Csillag dove wholeheartedly into a seemingly chaotic process of flip charts and sticky notes as we brainstormed early-stage chapter outlines. Shannon Auster-Weiss asked the tough questions about what each chapter was really about, did diligent research, and offered a fresh perspective, breakthrough insights, and upbeat energy that was contagious as we drafted the chapters. Lindsey Auster-Weiss provided creativity and wisdom in thinking about the cover and cheered us on throughout the process. Deep gratitude also to Lindsey Auster-Weiss, Shannon Auster-Weiss, and Steve Weiss for sharing love, laughter, and many moments of enlightenment—and for buying the awesome Mother's Day deck couch where much of this writing took place.

I am thankful to Carol Auster for all of her help with things in Canton during the writing of this book. Lisa Hillenbrand and Lesley Simpson shared life's ups and downs, swimming, and yoga and prompted me to think in new ways. Teresa Back streamlined Schulich work and offered her wonderful design expertise. Zippee and Shoji snuggled in and provided healthy distraction whenever I wrote at home, and Chip's sheer joyfulness on our morning jogs so often triggered a valuable thought or idea.

PART I

Understanding the Values Gap in Business

CHAPTER 1

The Values Gap
in Business

There is a values gap in business, and most businesses underperform because they cannot bridge that gap. The gap is not straightforward, and it is not as simple as *live your values and be authentic.*

First, all over the world there is a high degree of mistrust in business and its executives. Tell someone that you teach business ethics, and they have to manage not to laugh, or they say, "Oh, I didn't know business had any" or "Must be a short course." Public trust in business is at a low point around the world; and while a new story of business is emerging, it is dangerous for business as an institution to occupy the moral low ground in society.

Second, there can be a great deal of individual conflict around the idea of values. Values represent what is most important to us, and we often can be confused about these issues. In today's interconnected world, we encounter many difficult values issues that we have never before confronted. And sometimes we expect that values issues are simple and that if we just act on our values, our problems will be solved.

Finally, individual businesses have problems with making their values come alive in the organization so that executives and employees can act consistently in accordance with those values. And while many businesses have values statements, often they do not translate into living documents. Sometimes the business values conflict with one another, and sometimes they conflict with individual values of employees. Often the world changes, and companies encounter new situations that require rethinking how their values are relevant. The result of these forces is a values gap for many businesses.

Why Trust in Business Is at an All-Time Low

Enron was known for its innovative spirit and its commitment to a set of values called *RICE,* which stood for *respect, integrity, communication,* and *excellence.* Enron won *Fortune* magazine's America's Most Innovative Company award for six consecutive years, from 1995 to 2000. According to *Fortune,* "Famous for innovative thinking, Enron has led the charge for deregulation and consumer choice, and has created new businesses such as electricity trading, in which kilowatts are bought and sold like pork bellies."[1]

Yet even as Enron was reaping kudos on *Fortune's* Most Innovative Company list, there were allegations of massive fraud. In the businesses where the company was supposedly innovative, the numbers were misleading. There were also accusations of Enron's manipulating the electricity market in California. The board allowed the chief financial officer exceptions to the company's ethics policy so that debt could be moved into off-the-books special-purpose vehicles. The chairman and the chief executive officer (CEO) were convicted of criminal wrongdoing. Enron's accounting firm, Arthur Andersen, which shredded key documents, went out of business. Clearly, Enron had a values gap—and many have argued that Enron epitomizes what is wrong with business and capitalism.

Although Enron may be an outlier, there has been an unending cycle of business scandals, from the Teapot Dome scandal in the 1920s to the most recent financial sector meltdown. This cycle leads to a public perception of business as occupying the ethical low ground in society. Many people simply do not trust business as an institution that is able to better our lives. In fact, the surveys are pretty clear: public confidence in the institution of big business reached an all-time low in 2009, and in 2014 it remained at the bottom of the list, somewhere between organized labor and the US Congress.[2]

Think about recent history. Recall the headlines and news coverage of Enron, WorldCom, Parmalat, the United Nations Oil-for-Food Programme, Long-Term Capital Management, Bear Stearns, the tainted milk and meat scandals in China, the child labor of Nike, the Zimbabwe diamond scandal, and the raft of banks and former financial institutions that felt the pain of the global financial crisis.

One conclusion that some draw from stories of companies such as these is that business is not a trustworthy institution. After every scandal, critics cry for more integrity in business. After Enron both the *New York Times* and the *Wall Street Journal* urged President George W. Bush to support legislation to encourage auditors to be the primary guardians of business integrity to prevent fraud from occurring in the first place. These pundits have an underlying story about business that we call the "business sucks" story. They believe that business is an untrustworthy institution that drives the unrelenting pursuit of profits and self-interest and lacks any sense of values and ethics. They also believe that such greed and rapaciousness can be curbed only by greater forces such as government regulation.

What this point of view misses is the thousands of businesses that have never been tainted by scandal. For every Enron there are at least 10,000 companies employing ordinary human beings who are trying to do the right thing, creating value for those people the company can affect. It also does not account for the tremendous progress that companies have made in the past 35 years or so, paying attention to the communities where they are located, their effects on the environment, and their overall societal responsibilities and obligations.

A second and opposing reaction to the business scandals in the headlines is that our view of business is distorted by the media's penchant for sensationalism. After all, bad news sells. Some have reached this conclusion and suggested that we need to celebrate that business is devoid of emotion and rests on economic logic alone. They say that the emotional response of the media affects the average citizen but really has little effect on the real competitive world of business. This second conclusion is often hurled by those who want to agree that business is about the pursuit of profits but that if we have less intrusive roles than these other societal institutions, the search for profits will generate a better society. We call this underlying story the "business is great" story. Leave competitive markets alone, and everything will work out for the best over the long term.

This conclusion tends to ignore the fact that while many companies are out there trying to do the right thing, there are others that have caused some real harm in the name of "this is business." Of course, there are some bad apples like in any institution, but much of the harm done by the global financial crisis was in the name of finding innovative ways to conduct business and manage financial tools.

We are distrustful of both of these conclusions. Some businesses really do suck and some are great, but these politically motivated positions do not help us address what we believe is an even deeper problem that is much more difficult than a discussion of business scandals.

Business in the Twenty-First Century

Over the past 50 years, business has undergone significant shifts from its modern origin in the industrial age. Technology and globalization have radically changed the way we work. Many have argued that the physical routines that defined the industrial age are now irrelevant, at least in the West. Routine labor has been automated or contracted out to low-wage countries. There has been a well-documented shift from physical work to knowledge work, leaving many people behind. Companies have less loyalty to their workforces, and employees reciprocate in the face of layoffs and outsourcing. Globalization entails that companies think about their strategies in a worldwide context, complicating the nice, rational bureaucracies that emerged to run stable, domestic, industrialized companies that could engage in planning for a fairly predictable future. Those days are history for most companies.

The combination of incredible information technology and globalization has led to multiple disruptions in most companies. Often management responds by favoring the interests of one important stakeholder—the shareholders—over all others. Companies now live in the fishbowl of a 24/7 news cycle in which all of their actions are scrutinized. It's small wonder that public trust in business and its executives is at an all-time low.

Globalization also leads to exposure to many differing cultures that may interpret the same values in radically different ways; or they may be at very different stages of development, so issues long thought solved by the West become hot buttons in other parts of the world. Most Western societies have enacted prohibitions around child labor, believing that children must focus on their education, growth, and development.[3] Yet, as Nike and others have found, this view is not always shared around the world. Nike and its critics found plenty of evidence of child labor in the factories of its suppliers in Southeast Asia. And even though these were not Nike employees, the global news cycle ensured that Nike felt pressure to change the labor practices of its suppliers and its suppliers' suppliers.

Such cases are now commonplace, especially for businesses that have become iconic global brands. They are held accountable for everything that goes into the product, as well as the uses of the product and its disposal. The transformation of a global "value chain" into a global "responsibility chain" has occurred only within the past 25 years. Companies that try to manage this responsibility chain without a sense of what they stand for are headed for trouble.

Combine these effects of technology and globalization with the recent global financial crisis, and it's no wonder that trust in business and executives is at an all-time low and that many businesses are facing a values gap. Business neither sucks nor is great. Most businesses fall somewhere in the middle of that spectrum. Business leaders are struggling with navigating the complex world of technology and globalization and the recent global financial crisis amid negative portrayals of some of the companies that have derailed.

Business is too often seen as amoral, having nothing to do with morality and ethics. The common perception is that business is about only money and profits. Businesspeople are viewed as narrowly self-interested, unconcerned with anything but how much money they are going to make for themselves and their companies.

We believe that most of us want to lead and build businesses that are both inspiring places to work and beneficial to society. That means we need a more robust view of how individual human beings experience their business lives.

Business Is Also about Individual Human Beings

Angela got a phone call from Pierre, her boss's boss, asking her to come to his office immediately. When she arrived she found a few other members of the senior management team. Her boss, Jacob, was noticeably absent. Pierre asked Angela some sharp questions about Jacob and his top priorities for the team. Angela and her boss had their differences, but they had talked about them in a fairly open way, though Angela continued to believe that her boss had the organization heading in the wrong direction. She wanted to be true to her values. She wanted to answer truthfully, but she did not want to be a tattletale and disrespect her boss. She wanted to be authentic, but she was not sure what that meant in this circumstance. Angela experienced a real conflict in values. Her value of truthfulness and her value of privacy (not being a tattletale) were at odds with each other, and she did not know how to respond.

This case is typical of issues that nearly all of us face every day. We have values-related conflicts between work and family life and between our obligations and what we would prefer to be doing. Conflicts also arise when we are in novel situations. We may have a great set of values that we learned from our parents, but we have little idea how to apply them to twenty-first-century business situations inside companies.

Alternatively, we may be confused about what we really believe, or we may be at a transition point in life, where the waters ahead are very murky in terms of which values will persevere. Sometimes we have to rethink the purpose and meaning of life and decide whether or not to change course.

People are complicated. It is not so easy to just "act on our values," the cornerstone of living an authentic life. There are many barriers to living one's values, and being part of a complex company does not make things any easier. These conflicts contribute to the values gap for the organizations in which we work.

Taking Values Seriously

Sophie's first job after university was with a food distribution company in New Jersey that supplied products to boutique grocery stores in nearby New York City. She was excited and enthusiastic about her new position working in the human resources and organization development department. Sophie and her boss worked hard to build better relationships with unionized truck and forklift drivers in the factory where their offices were located. They believed that people should be empowered, and they thought that the company held this belief as one of its basic values.

Sophie and her team introduced progressive initiatives for the factory, such as increased flexibility in choosing shifts and the ability to bank two hours of time off for every hour of overtime worked. They renovated the lunchroom to be bright and cheery, with picnic tables and a patio outside. Shop stewards and the other employees were beginning to work with Sophie and her boss to solve other long-standing issues in the plant, providing creative input and suggestions for improving efficiency. Better protection for people working in the freezer department was also moving forward.

About that time Sophie was asked to hire 50 new truck drivers. She poured her heart into convincing folks that working for her company would be great, and she showcased all of its progressive initiatives. She was so convincing that many drivers left other well-paid jobs to join the company. Sophie oriented and welcomed these newcomers into the plant and worked hard to integrate them into the team. On the day before these employees would become union members, her boss's boss told her boss to tell her to fire every one of them. Clearly, there was a disconnect around the idea of employee empowerment that Sophie and her boss were developing and the firings that happened. There was a real values gap in this business.

Regardless of whether Sophie's company had a values statement about employee empowerment or a website that trumpeted the idea, the company was acting through Sophie and her boss as if this was an important value. Once the decision to fire people was made, however, the company's values were undermined.

Steeped in the old story of business, individual companies, executives, and employees often misunderstand how their business models are values-laden through and through. If we cannot bridge the values gap for individual businesses, it is highly unlikely that we can change the overall societal narrative about business and industry. And because much of our individual lives are spent in organizations, we need to address this business values gap if we are to deal with our own individual conflicts. It is more difficult than it appears for individual companies to get values right. Nowhere is this more apparent than in new studies of employee engagement.

In a recent worldwide survey of 142 countries, only 13 percent of employees said that they were engaged in their work.[4] Regardless of your political views of whether business sucks or is great, think about a business in which the vast majority of employees find little meaning and fulfillment in their work; they are unlikely to make contributions to their organizations beyond what is necessary to keep their jobs. Things are a little better in North American companies, where the engagement number stands at 29 percent, but that leaves 54 percent of workers not engaged and 18 percent who are actively disengaged.[5]

For many companies this means that more than half their workers just go through the motions. For another nearly 20 percent, they are not just hanging out but are actively checked out. Imagine getting up every morning and that is what you face: a job that is not engaging, day after day, week after week, year after year. This results in companies in which underperformance, waste, and human tragedy loom large.

Lest we paint too dark a picture, it is worth remembering that the story of business is rapidly changing. We see several important and simultaneous trends:

- The emergence of many values-based companies, such as Whole Foods Market, Google, Amazon, Facebook, Berrett-Koehler, The Container Store, and Novo Nordisk

- The rise of social entrepreneurship and the creation of innovative solutions for some of our most pressing societal problems through new social-sector organizations and by engaging employees and other stakeholders

- The push by traditional companies such as Unilever and others to remake themselves for the twenty-first century

As these trends accelerate, we need to be mindful about the temptation to think about companies in terms of saints and sinners. Inevitably, these "good" companies will make mistakes. It is tempting to invoke the old story and relegate them to the sinners category. Oscar Wilde is purported to have made the point quite succinctly: "Every saint has a past, and every sinner has a future."

Taking values seriously in a business is no guarantee of not making mistakes. The world is complex, and we need to be humble as human beings who cannot possibly know or predict what is going to happen. We can, however, figure out how to bring our values to life, how to infuse our companies and our business lives with what we stand for, and how to do values better. In short, we can bridge the values gap.

Toward a New Narrative for Business

In working with executives and businesses all over the world, we have learned that there are few truths that work everywhere for everyone. We have noticed that there is a growing movement to put values in the center of the way we think about business, and this is leading to a new story, a new narrative, about the purpose of business and how to be successful. Such a new narrative is integral to bridging the values gap.

Every business must create some value for its customers, suppliers, employees, communities, and financiers (the people with the money). These groups are a company's *stakeholders*. More businesses are recognizing that they must create value for *all* their stakeholders if they are to survive and thrive. Competition in a free society is very important because it gives everyone more options, but the basic question for any business is how it is going to make people's lives better so that they are willing to pay for its products and services.

This idea of stakeholders is often juxtaposed with the idea that business should be concerned only with profits and returns to shareholders. As every businessperson knows, however, this is a false dichotomy. Even if all you care about is creating value for your shareholders, how are you going to do it? You will need great products and services that create value for your customers (so they will pay you for them). You will need suppliers who want to innovate and improve your products and services or make them faster or cheaper or greener (so you will pay them for those products and services). You will need employees who are engaged in helping you understand how to grow your business successfully. You will need to be a good citizen in the community if for no other reason than to escape community regulation that might take value from your business model. And if you do these things well over time, you are going to make money. However you parse it, business is about creating value for its stakeholders.

We believe that values create value for stakeholders.[6] Doing values right energizes employees and other stakeholders as well. Great companies create value by relying on values. They figure out how to treat all of their stakeholders with respect and dignity, just like all of us want to be treated. And they infuse their business models with the very ethical values that we try to teach our children.

Entrepreneurs start companies because they want to somehow change the world. They have an idea that they want other people to benefit from. There are very few entrepreneurs, in our experience, who start a business solely to make money. Most of the great ones are fanatical or consumed with an idea. It is really pretty simple because the passion and purpose of entrepreneurs stem from their values. Great companies are built on passion and purpose and a set of underlying values in which people can believe. Much of the old narrative of business has forgotten this idea and has relied on the canard that making money is good enough. Even if that were true at some point in our history, it is not enough to sustain a business today.

Success in the twenty-first century requires that we avoid making tradeoffs among stakeholders. Instead we must deliver creative solutions to the difficult problems where stakeholder interests conflict and where there are conflicts in values. For example, great companies do not cut employee benefits to raise their stock price or screw their suppliers to keep prices low for customers. They figure out how the interests of employees, suppliers, customers, communities, and financiers converge in some kind of harmony over time. Of course, sometimes tradeoffs must be made, but great companies do not continuously make one group better off by making others worse off. Business is fundamentally a collaborative and cooperative enterprise. Indeed, we believe that business is actually the greatest system of societal cooperation that humans have ever invented. We simply misunderstand the underlying values that make capitalism possible.

One such value that we are increasingly becoming conscious of is that business is a deeply human institution, embedded within society rather than existing above it in some mythical free-market land where everyone is a short-term, purely economic maximizer. We are not merely economic beings but rather fully complicated humans with families, love relationships, and aspirations. We are economic and political and spiritual and more. To understand how business really works, we have to understand human beings and their hopes, dreams, and abilities to do great harm as well as good. Human beings are at least partially driven by their values—their sense of what is important for them to lead a meaningful life. There is no magical transformation of people into one-dimensional, greedy egotists when they walk into their workplaces. They do not check their values at the door and pick them up when they clock out.

The emergence of this new narrative prioritizes bridging the values gap. It will take a generation for the entirety of this new story to be worked out and realized. We are going to concentrate on one part of this new narrative: how to understand and bridge the values gap. If we can transform our businesses into places where we have an honest conversation about what is important to us, we can make our businesses fit for the twenty-first century. This requires a great deal of introspection and reflection. It also requires some frank assessments about the importance of our history, our connections with others, and our aspirations. Having these values conversations is precisely how to create an exciting, dynamic workplace in which people want to contribute and succeed.

In chapter 2 we further explore the individual conflicts in values because that is what all of us know best.

CHAPTER 2

Just Be Authentic: Not So Fast, Not So Easy

ormer Medtronic CEO Bill George gives some sage advice in his best-selling book *Authentic Leadership*.[1] He says that effective leadership is about being your true self—being authentic. Many leadership books presume that you can change leadership styles the way you can change your clothes, but most people know whether this is an act or a leader is being real. We can sense a mile away when people are faking it or pretending to be something they are not.

Being real and authentic to ourselves is what gets people to follow us. What does it mean to be authentic? The idea that we simply need to "walk the talk" is problematic. Sometimes we don't know what the "talk" is and sometimes we don't know how to "walk" it. Yet we all have a keen sense that being true to one's self is central to quality of life.

This is a very old idea. Recall Polonius's advice to his son, Laertes, in Shakespeare's *Hamlet*:

> *This above all: to thine own self be true,*
> *And...Thou canst be false to any man.*[2]

Follow your own values and everything else will take care of itself.

One reading of Shakespeare is that Polonius is quite a fool! He is giving fatherly advice to Laertes precisely because he has failed to establish any deep and meaningful connection with him. Their conversation is reduced to platitudes. We do not believe that values can be reduced to platitudes; rather we argue that such banalities create values gaps and are one of the main barriers to doing values right.

Hamlet is a paradigm case of a troubled person who is searching for what it means to be true to himself because he knows neither what his "self" is nor how to be true to it. By confronting his history, especially with his parents and their history; by examining his relationships with others; and by coming to terms with his own aspirations, he is able to gain insight into his own actions, and his life has a chance to be authentic. Hamlet suffers from what we call *the problem of authenticity.*

The Problem of Authenticity

Understanding ourselves and why we do what we do requires a commitment to being authentic, but being authentic is more difficult than it first appears. "Know thyself" is easy to say and hard to accomplish. We can start with what we think our values are, but we must be willing to engage in a dialogue with our past, our relationships with others, and our aspirations for the future.

There are many Prince Hamlets in the business world. In many cases, things just seem to happen and we go along, not bothering to understand who we are or what we are becoming. After a while acting authentically is either taken for granted or impossible. We need to get back to basics and understand what values really are, and we need to examine some key assumptions about the idea of self.

What Is a Value, Anyway?

It is difficult to give a definition of *values* that works for all situations. The search for general definitions often obscures the nuances that exist in most situations. One interpretation of a value is that it expresses our preferences. To say that respect is one of my values is to say that, all things being equal, I prefer to treat others with respect and that others treat me with respect. The power of this definition is that we can look at people's behavior and deduce whether they had a certain value. If I continually shout at people and call them names, my behavior says that I do not value respect, and it does not really matter what I am saying.

Understanding values as preferences expressed in our behavior makes the study of values easier. This definition underlies much of modern economic theory and social science. It has given rise to hundreds of empirical and quantitative studies of values, and it has yielded many insights about our ability to act rationally, in accordance with our preferences. More recently, this view has been used to show how our actual behavior deviates from some standard ideas about what would be rational.[3]

The problem with thinking about values as preferences in this simplistic way is that it fails to acknowledge that when we talk about values, we are talking about the things that are most important to us, not just our likes and dislikes. Values as preferences also suggests that each individual has his or her own set of unique preferences or values, which leads to many of the values gaps and barriers to doing values right. In addition, the idea of values as preferences is hard to critique. If we have a disagreement about values, we are just saying that we like different things. How is conversation to proceed from such a starting point?

Philosopher Edwin Hartman tries to remedy this problem by making an important addition to the idea of values as mere preferences. Hartman goes back to Aristotle and suggests that we think of values as relatively general and permanent ideas that capture our desires and preferences *after* we have engaged in some introspection. We do some soul-searching to determine the most important parts of our lives that are likely to persist over time. This is an important antidote to the idea that values are mere preferences. Values require introspection and reflection. While this may seem easy to say, it is difficult to do.

Hartman cautions us: "Most of us cannot state our values and their implications in a coherent and airtight way; hence unanswerable questions arise about whether we really hold this or that value… nobody is completely rational, we cannot always know whether a failure to act on a value is a failure of rationality, an absence of the value in question, or a simple lapse."[4]

There are additional problems with understanding values as preferences. The first is a problem of knowledge. If we could be sure of knowing our values—either our immediate preferences or our considered, rather permanent desires—things would be fine. The problem is we do not always know what these are, and sometimes we are not in the best position to discover them alone.

Think for a moment about a time when you said you believed in one thing but you aren't sure you acted on it. Human beings are simply rationalizing machines, and we need some checks and balances on our ability to gain insight into our own motivations. Sometimes we even deceive ourselves about our motives for action. We often need conversation with others who are willing to give us candid feedback about our behavior and why it is or is not consistent with what we say we stand for. And sometimes we actively mislead others about our values. We say one thing and then deliberately do the opposite. This is the hypocrisy behind "you aren't walking the talk" and "what's on the wall isn't what's in the hall." It is very difficult to tell whether people are making well-meaning mistakes or are actively trying to mislead others. Thinking about our values requires the consideration of and conversations with people to whom we are connected.

Values actually do change, and it is hard to sort out changing values from other motivations. As we grow and develop, we discover that what we thought was central to our narratives about ourselves really is not. Sometimes we find that what we thought we wanted actually changes and that our hopes and dreams have evolved into something very different over time. Values require us to think about our history and our aspirations. As we are exposed to other people and other cultures, we find that there may be different ways of doing things in the world that we have not yet thought of. And we find that even though we may share a value with people from a different culture, their way of realizing that value may be different from ours.

New technology can cause us to rethink our values, as well. Traditional values like respect for property and privacy have come under assault in the information age. Most of us who are of a certain age, and who learned about values and ethics from our parents and family, had no conversations when we were young about intellectual property. Property, for us, was "stuff," not a string of zeros and ones. We had no conversations about complex medical technology and when it should and should not be used. We had no conversations about downloading, piracy, and file sharing; and privacy was a very different animal than it is today. Technology has fundamentally shifted our understanding of values like property and privacy. Who is not confused about the actual meaning of these values in the twenty-first century?

We also tend to associate values with a set of words like *respect, integrity, caring,* and *responsibility.* Different values may be relevant at different stages of life. The teenager and the senior citizen experience the world in very different ways. One may have no real idea of the concept of a limited time on earth, whereas the other may have that context in front of her every day. These conflicts are especially prevalent in organizations where several generations of employees work together. A younger employee may well have a very different interpretation of a value like respect than does an older employee who grew up in a different time.

The most critical problem with the notion of values as preferences is that it tends to ignore that values are always set in some context, and it is the context that determines which values actually cause us to act in a particular way. It is not a matter of having a multistep decision process but rather a much more ambiguous idea of seeing oneself inside a particular situation, seeing the situation as a whole, and feeling the need to find a solution to a problem the situation brought about. Values as preferences, for all its strengths, does not do this process justice. So, the notion of values as preferences can at best be a partial solution to the question *What is a value?*

Philosopher Donald Davidson has tried to capture the concept of values as what is most important to us. He suggests that "values are answers to *why* questions."[5] This also captures the insight that we need reflection to discover them.

Suppose we ask you why you are reading this book. You might respond that you are interested in learning more about how values work in business organizations. We ask why you are interested in that topic, and you tell us that you want to become more effective as a business leader. We persist with the *why* questions, and you say that if you are a better leader, you can become more accomplished. Eventually, we will come to a place where you simply cannot answer anything other than "just because." Then we will have reached an important value, often called an *intrinsic value:* something that you value for its own sake. The other answers to our *why* questions may represent values as well, but they are extrinsic, meaning toward other ends. The point of *why* questions is to discover some important ends that need no further justification, at least for you. Your intrinsic values represent what is most enduringly important to you.

In summary we can say that values are part of the drivers of our behaviors and actions. They express our desires and preferences—especially if we have thought carefully about them—and they are answers to *why* questions. But that isn't all.

There are many *types* of values. We can think of personal values, societal values, and organizational values, and these levels form overlapping sets that can conflict. History is full of examples of conflicts between personal values and societal ones. We need only look at such issues as the denial of the right to vote for women in the United States. When such a conflict can yield a constructive conversation, often society changes, albeit sometimes too slowly. If there is no conversation about the value conflict, there is little chance for change. Silence breeds denial and contempt and can serve as the root of violence. Value conflicts are difficult to work out. They require imagination and at least mutual respect. Sometimes the lack of mutual respect at a societal level is an insurmountable problem.

Similarly, in the business world we have found countless examples of conflict between individual and corporate values. Recall Angela's and Sophie's situations in chapter 1. Often these conflicts are framed not in terms of the corporate values but of why a particular company does not really live its values. And if work is alienating enough, we hear people say things like, "Well, I didn't want to do that, but it's a business and I had to" and "I really don't believe in X, but I had to do it for my career." They depersonalize their actions and attribute them to "the business" or "the career" to create some distance between their behavior and their "self." It is precisely this idea of self that we need to examine more closely.

Values and the Idea of the Self

We have focused on the idea of values so far, but we need to also examine the idea that we all have one true self. We have an idea of our "self" as a kind of vessel that holds our values. This vessel is empty at birth, and we fill it as we grow and develop. Our values come to define us and our identity, and in the liberal West we take these values to be individualized. In many other parts of the world, the vessel is filled with values that are seen to be imparted from culture and society and are not necessarily so individual. We in the West are very proud of the fact that we can live together even if we have different sets of values.

This idea of the self, while containing much that is true and useful, has undergone a rather profound critique in recent years.[6] Some have argued that the very ideas of values and of self are linked. What we value is intimately connected to the boundaries we draw around our self, how we are connected to others, and how we describe our self and its aspirations. This is partially why we argue that the four aspects of values—introspective, historical, connectedness, and aspirational—must be seen as going together.

This notion of the self as a vessel for our individual values puts a premium on the idea that we are always free to choose what to do—and there is some truth in that notion, but it can go too far. We are connected together in our personal relationships as well as in society, and this individualized view of the self does not always capture the notion that humans are social animals who are very adept at engaging in cooperation. Relying too much on the idea of complete individual freedom makes us vulnerable to becoming estranged from the meaning that we attach to our activities with our fellow human beings.

Defining one's self and one's values is better thought of as a relational activity rather than an individualist one.[7] Values make sense to us because they allow us to act within a context where we are jointly creating meaning with other people. This is especially true in business.

We suggest that we need a view of the self that is an evolving self, a self that is engaged in a process of discovery of purpose, what is most important, who is most important, and how one wants to live one's life. We do not start out with a predetermined purpose. Some parents try to define a purpose for their children, but this often leads to unhappiness, rebellion, and psychological trauma. Purpose is to be determined or at least discovered as one grows and develops. Likewise, what is most important in life changes.

Think back to your teenage years and your preferences—your values and what you thought was most important to you. Are those things still true, or has your very idea of self evolved as you matured and developed? Even if as infants we start with a very focused idea of self, we know that this concept will change over time. Of course, our teenage values can help determine the kind of adult we become, but there is always the possibility of change and growth, and healthy human beings continue to grow and develop throughout their lives.

Clearly, who is most important changes as we go through life. We learn about who we are in part through our relationships—whom we love, whom we like to work with, and so on. Our values are connected to who is important in our lives, as well. And when we put these things together, we get an idea about how we want to live our lives that we are always able to revise.

Our selves and our values are interconnected, and there are several aspects that we must pay attention to if we are to live authentic lives. We begin with what we think our values are. The self as a vessel does not contain the answer for us; it is the beginning of a process. We try to explain or explicate our values—or at least what we would say they are now. This task is fairly easy to do.

We often ask people to write down the values that they want to teach their children as a way to begin this process. We then try to enlarge this idea of the self by being willing to reflect on those values and probe our past to get an understanding of how they have evolved. While reflection and introspection are necessary, they are not the be-all and end-all. And, as we will see in chapter 5, reflection and introspection are not simply matters of navel gazing. We also have to pay attention to context and history. What makes us unique as individuals? Without a hard, reflective look at where we are and where we have been, there is not much hope of resolving anything beyond a walk down memory lane. We have to pay close attention to the connections that enmesh us. We are at once individual selves and connected selves.

Sometimes we overstate the extent to which we are autonomous individuals, always with free choice in every moment and circumstance. In more-collectivist societies, people make the same mistake about being connected and having little choice. We prefer to think of the self as simultaneously autonomous and connected. The opportunity for living interesting and authentic lives comes from this conflicted way to frame the self. Finally, we realize that aspiration can grow out of this process of reflection, attention to history, and connection. We can figure out what we want to accomplish and how we want to live. We say more in later chapters about how this process works.

To summarize, values are about those ideas that are most important to us. Sometimes they do express our preferences. Sometimes they express our relatively permanent preferences after we have engaged in some introspection. Sometimes these preferences really motivate people. Value conflicts and tensions are inherent in interactions with others. They are embedded in families, work, cultures, and societies. Values are always part of experiencing a whole situation and feeling the need to do something about it. They require conversation. And to do values right requires that we see the self as able to change and evolve. Let's look at some examples that make these concepts easier to understand.

Authenticity and Values as a Process: Some Examples

Arjun was a student at a prestigious business school. In his last semester, he took a management course that had a reputation for giving students a very broad outlook on business. During the course Arjun realized that he did not really want to be an accountant, even though he had already secured a job with a top firm. By thinking through some of his history, he realized that he had always tried to do what his parents wanted him to do, namely going to business school and studying to be an accountant. He also realized that he did not want to spend his life in an accounting firm. Once he figured out that doing what his parents wanted was largely responsible for his accounting degree, he could admit that he loved to read and study philosophy and that he had ignored this desire for the years he had been in business school. He resolved to take more time in school and commit to majoring in philosophy to see what possibilities opened up for him. His parents and skeptical friends told him he would never get a job and that he would struggle the rest of his life, but, unlike when he was younger, he now knew that he had to follow his passion and do what was meaningful to him.

Arjun needed some answers to *why* questions, like *Why am I unsatisfied with where I am now and what I am about to embark on as a career?* He could get his answer only by turning to his individual history. Of course, there is nothing wrong with doing what your parents urge you to do, respecting their wishes, and preparing yourself to earn a living in a responsible way. These are perfectly good values, but each can have ramifications that may be difficult to realize. Because Arjun was not afraid to be introspective, especially about his history, he opened the door to a potentially more satisfying and fulfilling life.

Mark was an executive in a multinational corporation that was exceptionally bureaucratic and internally focused. He was proud of having worked for the company for years and having risen through the ranks. He kept pushing for the company to be more customer focused. Although he had made some strides and felt that people seemed to agree with him, there was a lot of apathy in the firm. Mark could not understand why people seemed to do only what they were told to do. He was constantly stressed and as a result was often aggressive. When he yelled, there was movement but no real action. Unfortunately, the stress got to Mark and severe health issues resulted.

Zoe graduated from business school with a great job at a prestigious firm in New York. Before business school she had worked for years in the creative arts. She tried to fit into the company culture, but her background in the arts was very much part of who she was as a person. She did a lot of soul-searching and talking with people who knew her pretty well—friends, professors, and family. She decided that she needed to choose a life that was more in line with her creative side. She became an entrepreneur and a writer, opening a yoga-teaching business and eventually writing an off-Broadway play. She is well on her way to becoming the full-time writer that she had envisioned. She had the good fortune to see that that aspiration was a result of how she connected with others, her own thoughts about her values, and her history.

Robert was enjoying the fruits of a great career in consulting. He was in his late twenties, traveling the world, and continuing to learn from his colleagues and clients. He was living his dream. And then his brother was killed in a car accident. The brother was 39 years old and had three small children. Even though Robert was not very close to his brother because of the age difference, this event caused him to think much more deeply about what "living the dream" really meant (introspection). Having grown up poor, was he living the consulting dream because he made more money than his family (history)? Was he doing this to please his parents, who constantly worried about money (history)? Did he want to have children and a family (connectedness)? Was his childhood dream to be a teacher ever going to be fulfilled (aspiration)? He decided to embark on a different career as a teacher, resulting in what for him has been a much more authentic life.

All of these people had admirable personal values, and each would have been able to articulate what those values were at some point in time. But just being able to say the words was not enough. Each needed to engage in introspection—difficult for Mark but easy for Arjun, Zoe, and Robert. They all needed to examine a set of *why* questions around their individual histories. They all needed to realize the set of connections in which they were enmeshed. Arjun and Robert did not realize how much family had shaped them, and Robert didn't see how important family was to him until tragedy struck. They all needed to recognize the links among their histories, connections, aspirations, and willingness to be introspective. In each case, this was an ongoing process.

Let us not make the mistake, however, of believing that every time someone decides on a new direction, that is more authentic than not. We know that some people constantly make pivots in their lives to avoid their history or connections. We think of people who engage in short-lived relationships to avoid dealing with the commitment that is often the foundation of deep and meaningful relationships. In business we often see standoffishness cast as being "professional" that prevents or disables authentic relationships from emerging.

Leading an authentic life is not merely stating one's values and trying to stick to them. At different points in time, we want different things in life. Circumstances change. We craft our own narratives about life and its meaning over time; and if we are honest with ourselves, we know that this process is difficult and not very smooth.

Leading an authentic life means struggling with change and with one's idea of self. We have aspirations for ourselves and for those connected to us, and we often fail to live up to those aspirations. Sometimes, through the lens of our values, we try to express these aspirations and our deepest hopes and dreams about how we want to live. Living authentically means asking hard questions and not always believing the answers that we want to give. It is about at once engaging our current values as best we understand them, constantly querying our past for clues about our idiosyncrasies and behaviors, engaging in conversations and relationships with others, and remaking our futures with our aspirations. And when we understand that we live most of our lives inside organizations that themselves have values, things become even more difficult.

CHAPTER 3

Authentic Organizations: Is Yours One?

The CEO of a large, successful, high-tech, fast-growth company wanted to start a conversation about the company's values. He had one of his executives, Linda, gather the top management team and hire a facilitator to provide some outside expertise. During the ensuing retreat, whenever the CEO raised his hand to talk, all the other hands went down. The team always deferred to the CEO and his point of view. When the CEO was out of the room, the team talked about a laundry list of issues and problems that were values related. In the CEO's presence, however, no one would say a word about those concerns.

The CEO had no clue about the effect he had on his team. The work environment was politicized, making honest conversation impossible. Further, in his closing remarks that day, the CEO reiterated that he would not tolerate corporate politics. When the facilitator asked Linda if the CEO was open to hearing that he was having a very negative effect on the company, she replied that the result of such a conversation would inevitably lead to her being fired. This company clearly had a values problem. There was not much authenticity. Today the company no longer exists.

In a different high-tech company, there had been trouble on a number of fronts. When the new CEO, Thomas, took over, morale was low, and there had been a number of high-profile cases of sexual harassment by some senior executives. Thomas expressed his disapproval of the way the company had handled the issue, and he pledged a zero-tolerance approach. To reinforce how serious he was, he gave out his private phone number to employees and urged them to use it if they felt sexually harassed. By putting personal action behind his words, Thomas gained immediate credibility and in a very short time was able to lead some frank conversations about a broader set of values for the company.

The Difficulty of Authentic Organizations

If being authentic as an individual is difficult, becoming an authentic organization can sometimes be overwhelming. After all, organizations can comprise thousands of individuals, and there is inevitable conflict among their values, no matter how much they share. To be truly committed to living their values, those in an organization must engage in a conversation about its purpose, aspirations, history, and connections to stakeholders. People must be willing to both reflect and act simultaneously.

In the previous example, Thomas knew that he had to act quickly to turn around the low morale. He knew that the issues were broader than sexual harassment. He embarked on a series of values conversations among all 7,000 employees, from the senior managers to the factory floor. It was important to structure the meetings so that everyone had a voice. Even more important was that each conversation led to a list of things that needed to be addressed. These became the responsibility of quality management teams. These values conversations worked because employees could see the results. Of course, the conversations did not stop at the initial meetings; the meetings actually empowered employees to bring up issues daily. Everyone knew that the organization was committed to getting better and living its values.

Shifting toward values as an opportunity to engage in dialogue about who we are, who we want to be and why, and how we should work together is more likely to result in the high-performing, thriving, innovating organizations we crave and strive for. The shift is not a matter of simply stating the company values, however, and then passing out cards and mouse pads and getting everyone aligned around the values. At the organizational level, there is even more complexity, and it is easy to make some fundamental mistakes, as we will see in chapter 4.

Part of the difficulty lies in the way we think about organizational values and the underlying story about what it means to be part of an organization. As pointed out earlier, there is a narrative about business that fundamentally constrains the authenticity of an organization: that business is always and only about money and profits. Even when executives listen to employees and empower them to make decisions, it is only with the aim of making money. This narrative also suggests that the only reason employees are motivated is because they want the extrinsic rewards of pay and benefits.

We have suggested that this narrative is mistaken. Of course, money and profits are important in business, but so is purpose. Employees work for extrinsic rewards, but the power of intrinsic rewards—finding meaning and accomplishing something in collaboration with others—is far more inspiring. This old narrative of business is slowly changing, but it can be a major barrier to living a company's values. For instance, whenever an organization makes a mistake (and all organizations make mistakes), critics often jump to the conclusion, "See, they really didn't mean those values. It's really about the money." By keeping the conversation about purpose and values alive and growing, companies can overcome the inherent skepticism in the traditional narrative.

Organizational values, like individual values, can be seen as the most important principles in the organization, as answers to questions like *Why are we doing what we are doing? How are we going to work together? Who are we creating value for?* and *Who cares about what we are doing?* We can think about them as trump cards that win the argument over other criteria.

In some organizations, such as DuPont, safety acts as a trump card. Whatever the organization does, it never compromises safety, and this is true for employees and other stakeholders who interact with DuPont.[1] While DuPont is known for safety, other companies have similar values that come from their histories and are part of the fabric of what it means to work there.

For The Body Shop, a cosmetics company originating in England in 1976 and now in 60 markets worldwide, the commitment to not use animal testing has been embedded in the company ethos from the start and is another such trump card. For The Body Shop, "no animal testing" means neither selling nor using ingredients or finished products that are tested on animals. Every one of its products is animal cruelty–free. This is one of the key values the company always upholds as it bring its "beauty with heart" mantra alive.[2]

In 2006 Nokia was the top producer of cell phones, enjoying roughly 50 percent of the market. Its phones stood for usability and reliability. Customer satisfaction and loyalty were high. Apple introduced the iPhone in 2007 and completely changed Nokia's fate, turning it into a marginal player that was later acquired by Microsoft. Many people think that Nokia's problem was a lack of innovation, but actually it was ahead of the industry. It was the first to invent a color touchscreen with a single button as well as the first to introduce the mobile Internet. Nokia was also the first to invent a tablet with a wireless connection and a touchscreen, but none of these innovations made it to customers. As it turned out, Nokia was unable to be consistent with its values to bring the innovations it produced to market.[3]

Contrast the response of Nokia with Samsung, which quickly challenged Apple's dominance and gained the reputation as a market leader as Apple stumbled a bit. Samsung offered more variety in smartphones, in both size and functionality, and its devices could be tailored to customer preferences. To get to that stage, Samsung had to first establish an innovation culture that was built on values. It reassessed its historical values and determined what was necessary to fulfill its purpose of being an industry leader. In the words of one executive:

> The complexity we are facing here is that both companies, Apple and Samsung, live up to their value of innovation. However, both companies also have a different interpretation of what that means in practice and how to put those values in place within their own companies. The real lesson with the Samsung case study is that the company did not shy away from fundamentally reassessing its company culture, identifying gaps, and investing in new skillsets that the board believed would be necessary to move to the next step.[4]

Samsung had to have the conversation about how to change its values; then it had to follow through and invest in the skills necessary to make that culture a reality. Values cannot be just words on a website; they live in the day-to-day processes of companies. And if those processes are not built on the values, there is a very wide values gap that is difficult to bridge.

Yet another issue that makes authenticity difficult for organizations is the existence of a web of authority relationships. We think of values, and being motivated by values, as coming from our hearts. Yet every organization has a power structure, and often people are simply told what to do and how to do it. Making this authority system run in the background so that people can be self-motivated by their values is difficult. In the worst cases, it leads to a superficial culture of values-talk, while the real motivation is in obeying the CEO's authority. Values are about having a choice and choosing to act on them.

All too often authority relationships become coercion and much is lost, but sometimes those conflicts are worked through.

This is especially difficult when the web of authority relationships spans the globe. Executives at a large US-based multinational consulting firm decided to commit to more of a work/life balance value for their consultants. The executives had noticed growing resentment among their consultants as it became a norm to work almost 80 hours per week. In one office the executive in charge stressed the importance of work/life balance and requested that managers be more efficient in planning projects and their milestones so that consultants need not work later than 9 p.m. He also requested that people come to work on time at 9 a.m. and not stay until the wee hours of the morning.

The consultants were hopeful of real change, yet the very next morning the executive in charge arrived more than an hour late, and soon thereafter managers began requesting that consultants stay until the early hours of the morning to finish work. Things reverted to old patterns, and there was no work/life balance. There were simply too many layers of management and too many differing interpretations of the value of work/life balance that the company could not realize the value. What started as a conversation about how to make the company a better and more productive work environment foundered on the multiple levels of authority that existed around the globe. Clearly, the company was unable to walk the talk.

When The Body Shop was acquired by The L'Oréal Group, the biggest cosmetics company in the industry and one that was engaged in animal testing, The Body Shop faced a value conflict that needed to be resolved. Executives managed to negotiate as part of the deal that The Body Shop would continue as a distinct brand and continue to commit to no animal testing within those product lines. What that meant for L'Oréal was that The Body Shop brands could not be sold in countries such as China, where animal testing of any cosmetic for human use is mandatory, even though they are massive markets. And, interestingly, The Body Shop philosophy has filtered into L'Oréal, which has invested heavily in researching alternatives to animal testing for product safety.

What is interesting about this story is that The Body Shop and L'Oréal found a solution that worked for both of them. Neither company had to completely compromise what it stood for. When companies force a value fit that might extend to their subsidiaries and suppliers as well, it often leads to even more serious problems.

When a Value-Fit Approach Leads to Empty Values

Many executives and organizations think about values in terms of the words and walking the talk. They try to find employees who say they have the same values as those claimed by the organization—thus seeking a fit between employee values and organizational values. Adopting such a value-fit approach generally focuses on two things:

- Trying to ensure that individuals and organizations live their values, that is, walk the talk

- Ensuring that individual and organizational values are aligned

While useful, the value-fit approach may not lead to the thriving organizations the executives were hoping for.

Take, for example, an organization with the stated value that its employees are its most important asset. In practice, however, employees are rarely consulted on decisions that affect them, and leaders focus predominately on maximizing productivity through efficiency-based approaches rather than more-inclusive approaches. Stories of workers being derailed or fired for voicing their ideas for improving the organization are told behind closed doors. Employees respond to this treatment by not speaking up, and sometimes they are complicit in the dysfunctional culture in the ways that they treat others because those are the behaviors the organization ultimately rewards.

Such an organization may post and preach its values, but everyday injustices lead to feelings of disenchantment, disillusionment, and stripped self-esteem among its employees. For some this disconnect erodes their passion and creativity and causes them to disengage, as they feel empty and unappreciated. Others, perhaps frustrated and angry that they lack opportunities for input or change, not surprisingly may either check out or undermine the company. Clearly, in this example both the individual and the organization are not living their values. Even though there might be a great deal of values-talk and superficial value fit, everyone knows that it is insincere.

On the other hand, when the individual and the organization are both living their values, there is enough alignment to start heading toward something better. If everyone is clear that it is all about profits and money, there is a degree of authenticity. In our view, however, value fit does not go far enough. We see it as a necessary first step.

The value-fit approach emphasizes the *content* of the values. This is where there is perhaps an agreement on values—but values are often static words that attempt to guide what we do. Fit is achieved by the organization recruiting on those values and enforcing them through such mechanisms as end-of-year reviews, annual retreats, training, and website and intranet posts. Values tend to be given or dictated. The emphasis is on whether alignment is achieved between individual action and stated organizational values. While there may be stability because both are aligned, there is also an opening for deception and bad faith. Simply living congruent values is unlikely to lead to thriving organizations.

We believe that it is better to see values as emerging through an ongoing conversation. Businesses are people joining together to act around a common purpose. What inspires, engages, and energizes people in organizations is not only what the stated values are but also the relationships, interactions, shared discoveries, collaborations, and pursuit of joint challenges and purpose in a changing world. To live creative and authentic lives, we need to do so in a context that is nurturing and supportive. For the authentic individual engaged in some introspective conversation about his or her history, connections, and aspirations, organizations must be places where this conversation does not get derailed.

Ideally, organizations can facilitate the growth and development of authentic individuals. People come together to understand their common history, connections, and aspirations. Such a joint process of ongoing dialogue about who we are, what we stand for, where we came from, and how we want to live in the organization nurtures the conditions in which authenticity is likely to emerge. We call this process in organizations *values through conversation (VTC)*. Instead of focusing on whether people have a particular set of values that are aligned with the stated organizational values, VTC focuses on the process by which we enrich and enlarge both individual and organizational values by engaging with one another to bring a conversation about values to life.

Starting the Values Conversation

Most people think that the way to start a conversation about values in a company is for senior management to decide what the values should be, issue some proclamation, and then make sure the new values are everywhere—on the walls and the website and the little values cards handed out when they are announced. Although there may be some benefits to this approach, it is also easy to make some mistakes. We talk more about these mistakes in chapter 4.

The Values Statement

In a multinational retail store, senior management had a difficult time saying what the company stood for. The company was routinely lauded for being well managed, and the executives insisted that they knew what its values were, even though they could not agree on how to state them. They became convinced that they needed a values statement to communicate the company's values to external stakeholders and new employees who did not know the company's history.

The CEO insisted on putting his own stamp on the values, and he had a direct connection to the company's founder. He had started at the very bottom of the company and had worked his way up to CEO, and he was very proud of the fact that the company tried to provide opportunities for everyone. He grudgingly agreed to get some validation of the values statement from the rank-and-file employees. After some focus groups that were generally supportive of the CEO's view, the values statement was turned over to the corporate communications group, which massaged the wording, made the values more generic, and then rolled them out in a series of cascading meetings from the top down.

There was some excitement that the company was finally articulating its values, but there was little follow-up other than a website. After four years the values were put into the performance appraisal system, but most people had forgotten the reason for establishing them in the first place. The value of providing opportunities for employees regardless of their background had somehow been lost. The company had a values statement, but there was little conversation about the values.

A large, complex bank had an alternative approach to focusing on the values statement. It had grown through mergers and acquisitions (M&As) for many years, and there had been many attempts to fuse the divergent cultures that resulted from values statements. The bank suffered from multiple platforms, differing cultures and expectations, and confused employees with low morale. When a new CEO took over, he was constantly asked when he was going to announce the new values that would be the foundation of his tenure. He responded that whatever those values turned out to be, the company needed to figure out how to give customers what they needed and how to make the bank a great place to work. If the company could not do that, articulating a set of words and calling them values would make no difference. Clearly, there was a values issue at this organization, but the CEO recognized that the problem would not be solved by yet another empty values statement.

All too often the values statement drives the conversation around values in an organization. Values statements are useful, but they must be the result of the outcomes of both conversations and behavior, which come first. The statements need to be grounded in both the reality of what a business is actually doing and in its aspiration to do better.

Unilever has struggled with these issues for many years. It recently made some breakthroughs by focusing its values on the behaviors it wants to bring about in the world. The company realized that its products touch the lives of billions of people every day, and it has articulated a vision statement:

> Our purpose is to make sustainable living commonplace. We work to create a better future every day, with brands and services that help people feel good, look good, and get more out of life....
>
> Our strategy for sustainable growth...sets out our clear and compelling vision to double the size of the business, while reducing our environmental footprint and increasing our positive social impact and gives life to our determination to build a sustainable business for the long term....
>
> By combining our multinational expertise with our deep roots in diverse local cultures, we're continuing to provide a range of products to suit a wealth of consumers. We're also strengthening our strong relationships in the emerging markets we believe will be significant for our future growth.
>
> And by leveraging our global reach and inspiring people to take small, everyday actions, we believe we can help make a big difference to the world.[5]

By focusing on the stakeholders that are actually touched by the business, Unilever adds realism to its aspiration. It states its vision in terms of actionable things that it is trying to do, rather than static words; it also integrates what are usually seen as business goals, such as "to double the size of the business, while reducing our environmental footprint and increasing our positive social impact," ensuring that it does not separate the business part from the values part.

The Role of Senior Executives and Entrepreneurs

We have suggested that the practice of having senior executives announce the values statement is at best questionable. What they *can* do is lead the conversation that comes *before* the values statement. The new CEO of the bank spent countless hours talking to people across the organization about how to have great products and services and make the company a great place to work. Leading a conversation is different from making a statement. It is tempting to issue the statement from the top down, since that seems like a tangible outcome, but when it short-circuits the necessary process it does more harm than good.

Most entrepreneurs start businesses because of their passion to somehow change the world. In the words of entrepreneur and Whole Foods Market co-founder and co-CEO John Mackey:

> Most entrepreneurs start businesses because they are on fire about an idea. Very few of them start a business solely to make money, except of course in economics textbooks. I have known hundreds of entrepreneurs in my life. With only a few exceptions, entrepreneurs didn't start their businesses to maximize profits for shareholders. Of course they wanted to make money, but that's not what was driving them. What was driving them in most cases was some kind of passion. They were on fire about something. It could be like Bill Gates wanting to create software to do the personal computer revolution. It could be the passion I felt with Whole Foods to sell healthy, organic, natural food to people.... The entrepreneur who creates the business is the first one to determine what the purpose of the business is.[6]

Part of the task of the entrepreneur and the senior leader in a large organization is to keep the purpose alive. As organizations grow, it is easy for inertia to set in as processes become routine and new people join the company. By constantly reminding employees of why the company exists, leaders can overcome this inertia and infuse energy into the organization. This is done not just with words but with a constant injection of new ideas, leaving room for the creativity of others in the process.

For John Mackey that creativity is particularly essential now. As fast followers are catching up to Whole Foods and cannibalizing its market share, Mackey has to work even harder to keep the company's values conversations alive. Under competitive pressure it is easy to shift gears and focus only on driving costs down because "that's what we need to do now," but in the process the real competitive advantage—the people and how they feel about the company—is often destroyed.

Tom Gardner, co-founder and CEO of The Motley Fool investment advisory firm, invented a process that helps employees stay personally engaged in the company's values. The stated purpose of The Motley Fool is *To Help The World Invest. Better.* The company states its core values thus:

Be Foolish!

- Collaborate: Do great things together.

- Innovate: Search for a better solution. Then top it!

- Fun: Revel in your work.

- Honest: Make us proud.

- Competitive: Play fair, play hard, play to win.

- Motley: Make Foolishness your own.
  Share your core value _____ .[7]

Every employee has his or her own "Motley value." It expresses the connection between that employee and the purpose and core values of the company. It gives the employees the message that their view really counts. In the words of Gardner:

> What we did is we assembled a group of people just to review our values—everything, even whether they felt that we had selected the right values. It was sort of a 10-year look back on our values: How much are we living by them? Are these the values that we believe in? Do we have the wording for the values? And are we expressing them and communicating them in our organization from somebody's first week at the company all the way through to their twentieth year at the company? How well are we doing? And that group came back with five or six recommendations, and one of those recommendations was the creation of our sixth value, which we call our "Motley value"; and, as you said, that's the value that you name for yourself.
>
> We're definitely a company that believes in self-expression, and we've found some unintended consequences of that. I can't say we would've predicted this, but naturally when you step back and think about it, it's true. If you can bring your own value, you're looking at how that value fits into the other values of the company, so now you're connecting with those values and evaluating which ones you think you live up to and which ones are challenges for you, so it has elevated the relevance of the values in our culture.[8]

Conclusion

It is difficult to make your organization more authentic. It is difficult to walk the talk, just as it is difficult to know what an organization's values really are. Business is complex in the twenty-first century, and it is too easy to look for a simplistic notion of fit to bridge the values gap. But fit is not enough. Values are more than words, and there is a great deal of conflict both within and between individuals and among the variety of interpretations of what the values mean.

What organizations need is a living conversation about values that is ongoing. In our experience, however, there are a number of key mistakes that can derail attempts to bring a conversation about values to life. In the next chapter, we explore some key mistakes about values to better understand them.

CHAPTER **4**

Do Values Right or Don't Do Them at All

J ust to throw down the gauntlet, we believe that most businesses are subject to something we call:

The Performance Challenge
Most organizations underperform because they don't
understand how values work. The challenge for organizations
is to do values right or don't do them at all.

To better understand this challenge, we discuss three issues: some common mistakes about values, the power of connecting values to the business model, and values through conversation.

Some Common Mistakes about Values

It is important to do values right for a simple reason: once you have framed a business model in terms of purpose and values, and once you have asked employees and other stakeholders to support those values, if you don't follow through, it is very difficult to get a second chance. This is not to say that employees don't forgive well-meaning mistakes, but they are much harder on hypocrisy. And depending on a company's history, employees can be brutal skeptics if new values or a new purpose is simply announced.

We want to share some of the most common mistakes that we have observed from our years of working with companies. In most cases, these were well-meaning mistakes, but they often led to deteriorated performance, morale issues, and increasing alienation of employees. Even when mistakes are well meaning, they can often be interpreted as hypocritical, especially if they are aimed at fixing morale issues.

The "Just Walk the Talk" Mistake

We hear this one all the time: "If you're serious about values, just stick to them. Do what you say you believe in." Some people have argued that while it may be difficult to know what your values are, once you do, most people are motivated to act in accordance with them. For these folks the "talk" may be hard but the "walk" is easy. Others believe that knowing your values is pretty easy. After all, they suggest, we learn values when we are children; they are reinforced daily by parents, caregivers, teachers, mentors, heroes, and others. The problem is that values compete with other motivations. Sometimes we are weak, and we lack the courage to do what we know we should do.

We think that both sides are correct here. It is increasingly difficult to know what our values are, especially in light of all the changes in the modern world in both business and our personal lives. We are bombarded with values issues daily that pose challenges to what we thought we believed, and all of us know that we are not always the best at sticking to our resolutions. Who has not claimed to value health but has had trouble sticking to a sensible diet? What company has not said that it wants to give the very best customer service yet has cut back on service when times get tough. Situations are complex, and rarely does a single value solve the problems that arise.

In some famous psychology experiments, social psychologist Stanley Milgram showed us how we can get so enmeshed in complex situations that a majority of us will actually deliver painful shocks to an innocent victim when told to do so by someone we believe is a legitimate authority.[1]

Values always have a situational context as well as a human context in all of its complexity. Saying "walk the talk," while in the right spirit, is just not enough. It is easy to say when we are on the outside of a problem, as a spectator; but when we are on the inside, with all the attendant emotions and pressures, it is much more difficult.

Values are more than words, so sometimes what is on the wall isn't what is in the hall. It is dangerous to assume that that everyone is on the same page about the meaning of words like *respect, teamwork,* and *integrity.* Think for a minute about your own top three values—or, better, the top three values you want to teach your children. What are they? We like to think that each person is different and has a unique set of values. This is only partly true. We have asked this question to thousands of people from multiple countries around the world, and we have found an amazing similarity in their answers. Most answer with some mixture of "integrity," "respect," "honesty," "responsibility," "caring," and "family." What counts as integrity in Virginia and Toronto, however, may be very different from what counts as integrity in Jakarta and Buenos Aires. Sometimes we use the words in different ways, and this is especially true in large multicultural and multinational organizations.

John, from Country Y, was a senior leader in an organization in Country X. Where John came from, *respect for others* meant being honest with them, even to the point of giving negative feedback. The culture of Country X was very different, and John said that "No one will be straight with me." The fact was that in Country X *respect* meant being deferential to one's seniors. John had to figure out how to get honest feedback and how to work through the different interpretations of what was meant by *respect.*

Getting the words right does not mean getting the values right. Many companies launch values programs by drafting what employees say they stand for. That draft is then handed off to the communications or public relations department to make the wording sound better as a published document. Often what happens is that key meanings and nuances are lost, the words come out sounding the same as those of every other company, and the power and impact of the values statement is negated.

The "Values Police" Mistake

Often what follows the establishment of a values statement is a discussion about how to build the values into a performance appraisal. This usually involves a rating of how well a manager or employee lives or models the values, and it often revolves around choosing the values that the employee best exemplifies and devising an action plan around those values on which the employee needs work.

At best this approach gives good feedback to employees about how they are perceived in terms of their values and suggests how they can improve. At worst people start acting like the values police or they pay too much attention to how they are perceived in terms of the values. They say things like, "I act on the values more than you do" or "That decision violates our values." They ignore the facts that values often conflict, that some decisions are difficult, and that sometimes situations are so complex that doing one's best is difficult. Doing values right turns into doing values righteously, and intolerance and conflict are the result.

The "Top Management Sets the Values" Mistake

The executives in a technology company went away for a strategy and vision retreat. They emerged with a set of values that they announced in a companywide meeting. They had convinced themselves that these values could reenergize the company and lead to better performance and more-meaningful work for employees. They were charged up and ready to go. The values fell flat on announcement, however, and the executives could not understand why.

After some interviews they discovered that the employees were on a different page. For example, the executives were energized by committing to the idea that *We have to earn the right to serve our customers every day.* They saw this as a way to emphasize that they needed to do a better job with customers and that they should not take customer support for granted. Some employees countered that that way of saying it seemed to devalue the work they were doing and had done with customers. They thought, *If I have to earn the right to serve customers every day, what about the past 10 years? Did that mean nothing?* They felt threatened. The executives had adapted a current buzzphrase that they wanted to "delight their customers." Some employees thought that this framing had a sexual connotation and was inappropriate. Obviously, the company's leaders needed a real conversation about what the company stood for and how they could say it in a way that was empowering and energizing for everyone, not just top management.

The "Better to Not Get Into It" Mistake

When someone says, "This is a values issue for me," they often mean to stop the conversation and take a stand. They often interpret values as etched in stone rather than meaning *We need to have a conversation.* This mistake often masks a conflict between employees' personal values and what they perceive are the company values. And it is precisely these kinds of issues that lead to disengagement in work. The response to "This is a values issue" is often a reluctance to pursue a conversation.

At a service firm, one employee refused to work with a particular client because "they have different values." One response, and often the correct one, is to respect the employee's wishes if there is no possibility of common ground. Many times, however, creativity and value can be created precisely because of the value differences.

Gina decided to accept a consulting assignment with a company in a controversial industry. She agreed more with critics of the company than she did with the company policy. Over time, however, she was able to get the company to sit down with its critics and begin to change its behavior. If Gina had simply said, "This is a values issue for me," the added value that was created would have been left on the table.

The "Values Are Soft and Fluffy" Mistake

If you think that values issues are soft and fluffy, we invite you to consider the most recent conversation that you had about values with your children, your parents, your friends, or your colleagues. Likely, there were some intense discussions about which values matter and how to live them. Businesses are often biased toward economic rationality, which is seen as objective and unemotional. Values are often seen as subjective and emotional. In reality, the facts of business are easier to address, and values conversations may be some of the more difficult discussions to tackle. Ironically, we have far more agreement among ourselves about values issues than we often do about so-called objective facts. For example, we are much more certain about the usefulness of telling the truth most of the time than we are about the latest economic forecasts.

Many believe that values are not subject to the same kinds of conversations as other elements of a business model, so what often happens after a process of stating values is that they are then rolled out. This is perhaps where most of the damage to values programs is done.

In a multinational energy company, values were rolled out continually, as each division, group, country, and other level had its own. There were so many mugs, mouse pads, sticky notes, and screen savers that it was difficult to tell what anyone believed. The company had more than 20 values, so employees did not know what was important, at least not through the values process. Management had let the communication of the values turn into a one-way conversation that stifled dissent and prevented employees from knowing whether the company was even serious about its values.

The "Values Conflict" Mistake

As mentioned earlier, sometimes we face situations in which values conflict, and we walk away without having had the conversations we needed to have to resolve the issues.

For instance, Jim wants to spend time coaching his son's baseball team, which requires him to leave work at 3 p.m. every day. Jim's company has a value around being in the office and available for everyone during business hours. One way for Jim to deal with the conflict is to prioritize the company's value of face time at work and resent the fact that the company prevents him from spending time with his son. Another way would be for Jim to have a conversation with the people in his division, seeking their input on how they could solve the problem together. Perhaps Jim's being available by phone or offering to do extra tasks during the evenings and weekends to take some of the burden off others would be an acceptable compromise. Even if they can find no way to accommodate both values, by having a conversation they can talk about what is really important to each of them and to their work as a unit. Our experience is that many businesspeople simply duck these tough conversations.

Another type of values conflict arises when employees face the pressure of competing company values. This conflict often occurs when we pay close attention to tough business situations. Most companies have a value around excellence in performance or superior customer service, and they also have a value around ethics or integrity or respect for employees. Unless we frame the situation as *How do we act on all of our values here?* these values can clash. If making the sales goal means an employee has to cheat, often the employee does nothing. Conflict can lead to paralysis. When we see values from a more holistic point of view—that is, as a living conversation about the important things in life and business—conflict can produce breakthroughs. We need to use our imaginations to find ways to satisfy all the values. For instance, how can we make the numbers without resorting to cheating? Or how do we push back against the target numbers? Again, values mistakes are often the result of a lack of an honest conversation.

The "Separation of Business and Values" Mistake

This mistake assumes that the business is separate from values and ethics. We often hear people say, "It's tough, but that's business." Or when someone in the world of sports is going to make a decision based only on money, you will hear them say, "It's a business." Indeed, this idea is embedded in the joke that *business ethics* is an oxymoron.

We believe that this separation is one of the main causes of underperformance. We are distinctly less than fully human if we have to think about our work as separate from living our lives as good people. The integration of work, where we spend more than one-third of our time, into the rest of our lives is important for healthy psychological functioning. And if that work can be construed as amoral at best, there is trouble. Spend one-third of your life ignoring the consequences of what you are doing to others, and it is likely that this bleeds over into your role as a parent, partner, and citizen.

Ethics and values must be integrated into business models. Understanding the links between ethics/values and business—and what we are trying to accomplish when we work with others to create value—is important. It illustrates the power of thinking about values through conversation.

Many executives fall prey to these common mistakes about values, making them from a position of goodwill while trying to do their best for their organizations and their employees. Values represent a very powerful way to lead organizations, and we want to emphasize that if we can connect our values to the organization's underlying business model, we are less likely to make these mistakes.

Connecting Values to the Business Model

There are several compelling reasons for connecting values to the business model in every company around the world:

- Values empower and engage employees.
- Values activate business strategy.
- Values are the wellspring for value creation.
- Values yield vision and purpose.
- Values lead to discipline, efficiency, and innovation.

Let's look at each of these.

Values Empower and Engage Employees

In the early 1980s, James E. Burke, CEO of Johnson & Johnson (J&J), led an effort to have conversations with employees around the world about the J&J credo, a set of values that had been passed down from the company's founder. Employees were urged to challenge the values: Where are we not living them? What processes and strategies do we need to change to live them more fully? Do we need to change the values? These "challenge meetings" were lively, and employees understood that the company was serious about living the credo.

Soon thereafter, in 1982, eight people died from taking Tylenol. The company's handling of the crisis, which was the result of tampering, has become a textbook case of good practice, and J&J was able to reintroduce the brand after voluntarily taking it off the shelves. Burke's view was that the employees were engaged in the business and built up a store of trust by what they did every day.[2] Because everyone knew that they were all on the same page about the values, the credo provided a high-level playbook for many different people to act seemingly in concert with one another.

Values, when companies actually mean them, are a powerful way to motivate employees to run the business in accordance with them. The values can act as a shield for employees to take action.

Jack, a young manager at a utility company, was in the field with a maintenance crew. He ordered a technician to fix something in a very dangerous way. The technician pointed to the company's slogan about safety that was on his toolbox, and said, "You can't make me do that," saving himself from a dangerous situation and, according to Jack, saving Jack's career. Alternatively, if "safety" had been mere lip service, imagine the possibility for disaster. This is why we say, "Do values right or don't do them at all."

Values Activate Business Strategy

Novo Nordisk is an insulin company that is built on values and a commitment to creating value for its key stakeholders. The company puts "people with diabetes," not "customers," at the center of its focus and is committed to wiping out the disease. This picture is important because it yields more than a business strategy of looking for existing markets. In some parts of the world, diabetes is much more of a scourge than even HIV (the human immunodeficiency virus). Novo Nordisk has had to figure out how to get insulin to people who cannot afford it, who cannot refrigerate it, and who do not even know they are diabetic. It is the company's values that activate such strategies.

Peter Drucker, a management consultant, educator, and author, once said that one of the most important questions that executives should ask is *What business are you in?* We want to add another question to this good advice: *What do you stand for?* If you are as clear as you can be about the answer to this question—and that is not easy (but we offer guidance in chapter 7)—it will help determine what business you are in.

Values Are the Wellspring for Value Creation

Values help us answer not only what we stand for but also for whom we want to create value and how we do that. Focusing on creating value only for shareholders ignores what actually happens in business.

Husk Power Systems is a startup company in India whose purpose was to provide affordable electricity to rural villages in underdeveloped areas, beginning in Bihar, a very poor state. Husk empowered local entrepreneurs to run the businesses and was successful to some degree for its first few years, but senior executives realized that something was missing. They could not seem to get to the next level. They were focused only on making electricity affordable to poor people. They determined that they needed to rethink their aspirations. They discovered that customers wanted more than access to electricity: they wanted to have it on demand, not just for a few hours every day. Husk actually had to change its purpose; and when it did, the company really took off. The executives raised their expectations and aspirations, and they activated their employees.

Values Yield Vision and Purpose

When we act on our values in an intentional way, we are committing to them by our actions. As we increasingly identify what we think is required to live those values, it is easier for vision and purpose to emerge. We believe that vision and purpose are best considered as emergent and evolving phenomena rather than as an pronouncement, as at many companies. By taking a hard look at our own behavior, as we will argue is necessary through values conversations, we can more easily see what we have to do if we are to serve as examples to our children, our community, and our employees.

Acting on our values rarely involves acting alone. If we are serious about vision and purpose, we must marshal the support of others who may not be as committed, again pointing out the work that is necessary.

Values Lead to Discipline, Efficiency, and Innovation

Another benefit of acting on values is that they serve as a means to discipline ourselves. Best-selling author Jim Collins found that the companies that were "built to last" were most often built on a set of values and purposes that did not vary over time. He hypothesized that the benefits of these values were discipline, efficiency, and innovation.[3]

Discipline results from being committed to the values and not accepting big deviations from them, though interpretations of the values could change. Efficiency results because everyone is on the same page. Values, like trust, yield efficiency without the bureaucratic costs. For instance, we may not need many rules about travel policies because we know that everyone is on the same page about giving our customers the best price. And because sometimes values can conflict and circumstances can change, we need to be open to new ways of thinking about our values, and hence innovation results.

Toward Values through Conversation

We have observed many individuals and companies struggling with values issues, making some of the mistakes we have outlined in this chapter as well as benefitting from the power of values-based leadership. We believe that the easiest way to overcome some of the problems inherent in trying to build a values-based business is to bring to life a conversation about values. Living one's values, as an individual and as an organization, is better thought of as a process that is reflective and recursive. We try to do it, get some feedback, reflect on it, and improve next time.

Becoming a more authentic organization is a continuous process. There are a few rules of thumb that seem to work. Values through conversation is not a program to be rolled out. It requires building a commitment to being authentic, to narrowing any values gap that exists, and to getting more people to bring more of their authentic selves to work every day.

Becoming more authentic must involve everyone in the conversation about values. Many people in organizations are simply not engaged in or are actively disengaged from their work. There are many ways to get more engagement, and research shows that performance is directly related to employee engagement, passion, and inspiration.[4]

Involving everyone in a conversation about what is important is a surefire way to increase engagement; however, one caution is in order: you must be willing to listen and respond to what employees are saying. We have seen countless values conversations flounder because the senior executives knew they had to involve many levels of employees, but they didn't really want to hear what they had to say. In those cases, VTC lessens engagement because employees can smell the hypocrisy.

Part of involving people and listening to them is encouraging them to push back. Indeed, we believe that this may be the biggest reason why values conversations often fail. Executives do not often encourage enough pushback. In the words of one CEO, "You tell people that your door is open, that you want feedback, that you want to be told when you're about to do something stupid. Maybe 10 percent will do it."

Another CEO told us, "I have to leave early today to meet with an employee who I'm sure is just a troublemaker; but if I don't meet with him, others won't be willing to come forward when there is real stuff I ought to know about."

Encouraging pushback is more difficult than it seems, especially in systems of authority and power. Many companies have installed hotlines, ombudspersons, and other anonymous means of conveying information. Common sense (and research) tells us that people are hesitant to use these processes, especially if they are already disengaged from the organization.

We are all human, and we often don't want to hear bad news. We also don't want to disappoint others, especially bosses, by giving them bad news, so there is a built-in bias in organizations to discount data that disconfirm a positive outlook. Often executives ask for feedback on their own behavior or leadership, but the request comes across as seeking praise rather than honest feedback.

One executive we are familiar with simply could not accept any negative feedback or critique of anything about the organization or himself as a leader. He had worked long and hard, night and day for the company for more than 35 years, and he saw himself as the personification of the organization. Any criticism shared with him he saw as a personal and disrespectful blow to himself and all he had built. He would yell and rant and deny. It should come as no surprise that after a number of attempts, most people simply stopped giving him anything but praise. Interestingly, the few who had the courage to push back often saw their ideas move forward, even if he took credit for the ideas himself.

Executives must make a personal commitment to pushback, both asking for it and giving it to their superiors. Being a role model is the surest way. We are fond of the motto *If you can't deal with the feedback, don't ask for it.*

Values conversations can be difficult. Sometimes we cannot find a way to resolve conflict. If the conversation is to stay alive, we have to acknowledge that at times there will be gridlock. The conversations take time and do not always lead to agreement. Some organizations reach an impasse, and it is important to acknowledge when this happens. Often such stalemates emerge when management and labor are estranged and neither believes that the other side has anything but narrow self-interest at stake. There are solutions to these types of situations, too: We can listen and acknowledge different points of view. We can try to agree on upcoming processes for working through. And we can stay committed to continued conversations.

There is a misconception that conflict has to destroy value for someone, that there must be compromise on the part of at least one party. Our experience, however, is that conflict, under the right conditions, is a wellspring of creativity and innovation. If an organization is committed to creating value for its stakeholders, conflict among stakeholders offers the opportunity to conceptualize the possibilities and relationships so that both parties win.

When an organization begins to work on its values and purpose, there is a tendency to look "future forward." This misses the opportunity to engage people about their achievements and feelings of pride. Acknowledging and celebrating past successes and the effort that went into them goes a long way toward helping people let go and look to the future. Forcing the future without saying good-bye to the past often creates resistance that takes a long time to reverse.

As companies undertake work on their values, it is important to look outside the organization. Many companies stumble by not involving external stakeholders. Living one's values involves understanding customers, suppliers, financiers, and communities as well as employees.

Whole Foods Market probably takes stakeholder involvement as far as anyone. Processes for involving stakeholders are woven into the company's daily routines, and it also involves stakeholders in the bigger picture. Every three years the leadership invites stakeholder representatives to a multiday meeting to talk about the big ideas that worked, those that did not work, and those that should be changed or abandoned. The executives gather stakeholder input about the current values statement.

Many businesspeople are afraid to involve stakeholders beyond a certain degree because they believe that confidential information will become public. There are very few secrets in today's global and tech-driven world, however, and the benefits of authentic relationships with key stakeholders far outweigh any revelations that may occur.

Many executives believe that they are great leaders because people tend to follow them. They fail to distinguish between *leading from a position* and *leading by choice*. People will naturally follow someone because of his or her authority. We need only look to human history to see both good and bad instances of this principle. Leading by choice is different. The leader by choice wants people to choose to follow. This means they must have knowledge of the leader's program and values, and they must have alternatives. Getting people to choose to follow inside a system of authority is difficult. In working on values, executives must be cognizant of this distinction. Authority exists in authentic organizations, but so does choice.

Leading or enabling a values conversation is one of the most important executive skills, and it is often left out of executive development. Because values signify the most significant areas of our lives, we are hesitant to share them with others. In the West our individualist cultures make us reluctant to criticize and offer feedback to others because each is seen as the master of his or her own values.

Conclusion

There are common mistakes that many companies make when trying to bring to life a conversation about values. If executives can avoid these mistakes, connecting values to the business model represents a very powerful management tool. By paying attention to these practices, executives can lead a conversation about values. Such conversations must simultaneously address the organization's ability to be introspective and reflect on its historical context, its capability to foster connections among employees and stakeholders, and its aspirations and purpose.

Throughout the rest of this book, we develop the details of values through conversation. It is not a complicated idea. In fact, all of us as parents know how to do it. We teach our children values through conversation from the time they are very young. We talk to them, give them examples, and try to be role models; and we talk about mistakes and what could have been done differently. We need to bring this expertise into our organizations.

There are four interconnected aspects to this process, and sometimes we refer to these as values themselves.

First, there must be a willingness to reflect and be introspective. This is more difficult than it sounds because we need to pay attention not only to ourselves and our thoughts but also to what others are saying about us. We refer to the values that drive self- and collective reflection as *introspective values*.

Second, we need to pay attention to our history. So much of what we do as adults is unconsciously connected to our own individual past, and there is much that we can learn about ourselves by taking an honest look. We refer to the historical part of the process as *historical values*.

Third, we need to acknowledge and understand the power of connection to others. Human beings are social animals. We do not live alone and we never have. Indeed, our language has developed in part so that we can achieve a great deal with our fellow human beings. This part of the conversation we call *connectedness values*.

Finally, we have aspirations, hopes, and dreams that we want to accomplish, lives that we want to lead. These *aspirational values* can often grow out of the other parts of the conversation, and in fact we argue that this is a better way to keep the conversation alive. At different parts of our lives, our aspirations change, so seeing aspirational values as an outcome of introspection, history, and connectedness retains the possibility of growth and development.

To explain VTC in more detail, we turn to the task of understanding how we can become more authentic as individuals and businesses by adopting this process view of values.

PART II

How Businesses Can Bridge the Values Gap

CHAPTER 5

Introspective Values: Reflecting on Self and the Organization

In a $100 million company with multiple lines of business from food service to hotels, every Monday morning the senior management team would meet and the CEO would ask each business unit manager to report on the results of the previous week. Whenever there was any bad news, the CEO would demand to know what happened. Oftentimes no one knew why, for example, sales had dropped by 5 percent, so the business unit manager would find some excuse, and sometimes a real reason, so as not to be embarrassed in front of the others. Among the business unit managers, this became a game that they willingly talked about among themselves. The CEO never understood that by threatening public embarrassment and by asking questions that did not have meaningful answers, he was causing his team to be unreflective and to actively engage in the search for excuses instead of real actionable causes.

The Role of Introspection in Values through Conversation

Take a pause. Look forward. Look backward. Look sideways. Look up the hierarchy. Look down. Now start having conversations. What do

AT A GLANCE: INTROSPECTIVE VALUES

Bridging the values gap through self- and collective reflection on how everyday decisions and actions facilitate or impede living our values successfully

Benefits

- Learn from what we do
- Recognize blind spots
- Avoid reinventing the wheel
- Find untapped markets
- Share and reapply practices and processes
- Personal and collective renewal

Principles

- Embed introspection into everyday processes
- Outward introspection
- Introspection as an ongoing journey

Practices

- Run pilots and experiments
- Engage in ongoing external monitoring and assessment
- Create check-ins and pulse checks
- Do pre-mortems and after-action reviews
- Try appreciations

we learn? Where are we going? Do our recent choices still make sense? Most businesses spend a lot of time focused on current goals and firefighting activities that leave little time for reflection. The annual strategic-planning retreat or the quarterly have-we-met-our-targets? meetings may trigger a bit of contemplation, but typically these activities are intermittent and future oriented. By being so preoccupied with the present with only an occasional look to the future, there is little time for introspection on how everyday and taken-for-granted decisions, actions, and behaviors facilitate or create barriers to success and narrow or widen the values gap.

If we are to bring values to life through intentional conversations—what we call *values through conversation*—reflection and introspection must be part of the process. Focusing on introspection and introspective values can uncover blind spots.[1] It can also help us understand the consequences of our decisions both inside and outside the organization. VTC enables processes of self-discovery and self-development that allow us to better embrace the vision of our organizations and determine how to realize our strategic goals. Conversations about why we choose particular courses of action can shed light on our underlying mind-sets and how we think. Introspection leads not only to self-understanding but also to conversations with stakeholders about our own behavior. Are we living up to their expectations or failing on some things? By valuing introspection, reflection, and their related values, we can find strong internal motives for self-improvement.

Using these introspective values might mean being curious, temporarily removing judgment and preconceptions, and adopting *shoshin,* what Zen Buddhists call a "beginner's mind." Even if we think we are experts, by viewing our surroundings and actions with a beginner's mind we see our behavior with a new perspective. In many organizations there is often little questioning or probing of alternative points of view. Power often trumps honest conversations with those at lower levels who may be fearful of voicing their true opinions and insights. Truly great companies have a built-in value of dissent—a broader notion of a willingness to ask hard questions about why the organization is doing what it is doing, stepping into the shoes of stakeholders, and approaching those discussions with an open mind.

Introspection also helps us figure out what to let go of, what to stop doing and say no to, as well as what to move forward with and say maybe or yes to. It helps us understand what we need to keep doing or stop doing and what we need to create that does not currently exist. By seeking dialogue and feedback, we gain an outside-in perspective that enables us to see ourselves as others do and avoid navel-gazing mishaps. Such an introspective attitude is a precursor of building a sustainable, high-performing organization.

The Benefits of Introspection and Reflection

Many benefits can be gained from examining and reflecting on our decision-making process, our purpose, our aspirations, and even seemingly mundane tasks such as how to improve our meetings. Part of growth is learning, and often learning stems from introspection of the organization's purpose and values, just as there are personal benefits of reflecting on our own values and on the world around us. These benefits include breakthrough insights, learning from our mistakes and those of other organizations, sharing best and next practices, avoiding duplication, discovering opportunities for reapplication, and allowing time for restoration and renewal.

It is easy to be caught up in quarterly pressures and pay attention only to our volume of sales or monthly reporting; and in the process and often without noticing, innovation or customer service may dip. Companies that do so typically do not sustain success. When values conversations do not include introspection, we are on a fast track to what only looks like success, and we never pause, contemplate, look back, or really look forward. We make rash decisions, often reinvent the wheel, fail to learn from what we do, repeat our mistakes, and miss the opportunity to leverage what is working well.

Creating space for reflection and introspection helps facilitate success in organizations much as it does for individuals. Critical shortcomings are uncovered. These conversations focus not on casting blame or pointing fingers but on working together to solve issues and move forward. That requires transparency and being in tune with ourselves. Are we wearing rose-colored glasses, overlooking our limitations, or distorting what is happening beyond the C-suite? It is easy to do if we are not building in introspection, and it is often tough to transcend.

Traditional satisfaction or employee surveys may provide some insights, but such instruments often fail to reveal the real issues that are simply not discussed in the organization. Similarly, 360-degree feedback, although seemingly a good idea, may also be distorted, with employees worried that giving feedback will somehow come back to haunt them. And, as Susan Scott notes, who really wants anonymous feedback anyway?[2] Wouldn't that make us a bit paranoid? Wouldn't we want to have a conversation with someone giving us positive or negative feedback?

Getting real feedback from stakeholders is an essential foundation for introspection. A recent McKinsey study of 52,240 individuals at 44 companies found that in 70 percent of the participating organizations there were gaps in how individuals filling different job levels viewed certain behaviors and experiences. In addition, in more than 60 percent of the companies, C-suite teams were much more positive about their own leadership skills than was the rest of the organization.[3] This data suggest that systematic and rigorous introspection, including conversations with stakeholders, will provide some unexpected insights for top leaders and the entire organization and will uncover some of the muffled voices and the elephants in the room that we often cannot hear or will not discuss.

VTC Principles and Practices: Bridging the Values Gap by Bringing Introspective Values to Life

Introspection might include a team's asking itself how the work it is doing, such as specific activities or projects, translates values into action; or it might include a discussion of how the team is—or is not— living the values on a personal level. These are tough questions about when and how certain values apply and which ones do not. Equally important are questions that delve into the shared understanding of those values and how that understanding can evolve. Deeper introspection might expose the organization's common assumptions as well as routines, norms, and processes that have become habitual. Few people, if any, may know why these routines were implemented in the first place and why they are perpetuated.

A classic example of the power of unexamined routines occurred during the 1962 Cuban Missile Crisis.[4] The Soviets had put missiles in Cuba, just 90 miles away from their enemy the United States. The US Air Force discovered the missiles in part because they were in trapezoidal patterns, typical of Soviet missile placements. The Soviets were unaware that their procedures and habits made them discoverable to their enemy.

Raising awareness of habits and their effects is one aspect of how working together on introspective values can shed light. Introspective conversations and appreciative inquiry can also uncover the things that are working well in organizations—things that often go unnoticed because they are running smoothly. From that insight companies can think about whether those positive actions might be amplified or diffused. Introspection also brings to light problems and issues that are festering or soon to escalate.

Introspection will look different in every organization, but there are some success principles and practices for introspective conversations that are often found in thriving organizations, such as Harley-Davidson, Procter & Gamble, Kaiser Permanente, Schlumberger, Apple, Best Buy, and Free The Children.

Embed Introspection into Everyday Processes

Companies can leverage introspective VTC by building in systematic time for reflection organizationally and individually. Organizationally, we can run small pilots and experiments and learn from them before committing large amounts of resources to a course of action. We can do pre-mortems before launches to force us to think through what might happen and make contingency plans. Pre-mortems might mean fast-forwarding six months and asking if the project succeeded and what led to that success or, if the project failed, why it did.

For example, NASA continuously trains its astronauts with extreme pre-mortems in the form of space simulations. As Chris Hadfield, a highly decorated astronaut who has flown about 2,336 orbits around earth and 62 million miles and spent five months on the International Space Station explains, a heavy component of space training is preparing for the worst so that you don't panic.[5] In many space simulations, not only are planned curve balls thrown in but there are also "green cards"—totally unexpected, randomly triggered crises often in conjunction with other extremes. This ensures that by the time astronauts are headed to space, they feel confident that they can cope with virtually anything that might occur.

Hadfield calls this the "power of negative thinking." "Death sims," as he calls them, are "weirdly uplifting." Play-acting catastrophe scenarios day after day enables astronauts like Hadfield to know that they have problem-solving skills to deal with the unexpected. These death sims also significantly lessen worries that might keep the astronauts up at night. Careful thinking and introspection about possible scenarios is essential for a safe and successful space journey. The same is true for organizations: anticipatory introspection can often reveal valuable information that can be preemptively managed or that may prompt us to make different, better choices.

Introspective VTC might also involve taking a hard look at customer feedback or immersing with customers in 24- or 48-hour customer *anthropological dives*—in-depth consultations with customers to learn how they use products and to glean valuable insights. Systematic introspection might also trigger movement toward more holistic and systemic action rather than temporary solutions. It might trigger responses to challenges or uncover positive results that could be replicated and reapplied.

We also can make after-action reviews (AARs) part of every initiative and project we launch, thus creating space for VTC and discussions about whether we are living our values. Harley-Davidson has been doing AARs for years. They may range from simple "I love, I wish, we should," as done at Procter & Gamble, or *plus/delta,* another common AAR in which + captures what was good and Δ indicates what to change the next time something similar is undertaken. AARs might also take the form of focus groups, more open-ended input, or more-detailed quantitative analyses and surveys. Whatever the format and process, just like pre-mortems, conducting AARs brings introspective values to life and is an opportunity to reflect, document, share, learn, and provide useful feedback for others.

In addition to capturing these reflections, creating mechanisms for posting and leveraging the insights has many benefits. For example, the US Army, founding originator of AARs, captures all the learnings from its postmortems in the Center for Army Lessons Learned (CALL). Introspection might also include "appreciations" that companies such as Whole Foods Market and The Container Store engage in at the start or end of meetings or projects, wherein each person reflects and shares something that he or she is grateful for in another member of the team. Such seemingly simple introspections also build community within the organization, which we delve into in chapter 7.

Kaiser Permanente (KP) is the largest American nonprofit, nongovernmental healthcare delivery system. It is a fully integrated hospital–doctor–insurance company model that prides itself on being an "accountable care organization" on steroids, with nearly 200,000 employees and 17,000 physicians working on behalf of 9 million members and patients to the tune of more than $50 billion in annual revenues.

Former Chairman and CEO George Halverson says that introspection is the glue that bonds the organization:

> The collective pursuit of continuous improvement is powerful not only because of the performance gains it yields, but also... because it's the only cultural value that could unify an organization as large and diverse as ours....By emphasizing a value we share and can all act on, we create a strong sense of "us."

> ...Three conditions must exist: People must have a rational understanding of how small improvements compound to make big differences. They must love improving—both because they are passionate about the importance of their work and because it feels so good to move to a new level of performance. And they must have enough confidence in their colleagues to believe that the organization is capable of making progress.[6]

Through its "innovation consultancy," a dedicated team whose purpose is to generate breakthrough ideas for better patient care, KP reaches out to stakeholders to reflect on and discuss what is working or not and how it can be improved. Mismanaged medication is one of the most common causes of lengthened stays, disability, and death in hospitals. A simple but effective solution that KP discovered through conversations with nurses and patients is the No Interruption Wear (NIW) sash or vest that is worn by a nurse while dispensing medicine to patients to signal that he or she should be not interrupted. Similarly, patient care areas have a marked space, the "Sacred Zone," which focuses exclusively on medicine pouring and dispensing.[7]

In Hawaii, KP introduced the first-ever mobile medical vehicle, increasing medical care access to remote communities, where health disparities are often greatest. The 500-square-foot, 10-wheel vehicle is staffed by a mobile health team, including a nurse practitioner, a medical assistant, and a mammography technologist, with physician services also available. This is just one of KP's mobile health initiatives.

In the continental United States, mobile vehicles are delivering health-care screening and services to workplaces in a number of states.

KP also launched Skype appointments with doctors and is optimizing the use of smartphone technology so that patients can receive medical help without leaving their homes. All of these initiatives are examples of how KP engages in introspective VTC, listening and reflecting on the feedback it receives and the data it collects to better bring its values to life.

As KP's current CEO, Bernard Tyson, notes, unlike many hospitals that maximize hospital days to increase revenue, Kaiser Permanente takes to heart its mission "to provide high-quality, affordable health care services and to improve the health of our members and the communities we serve."[8] In the hospital industry, pressure ulcers (bedsores) are a very accurate measure of how patients are treated. The industry average is 7 percent. Kaiser Permanente, in contrast, has the lowest number of pressure ulcers in the industry, at less than 1 percent.

Introspection might also involve reflecting and capturing problem-solving solutions. For example, Schlumberger has InTouch, a proprietary technical support service for field operators on oilrigs. The InTouch database, which contains more than 1 million knowledge items and receives 8 million views per year, is managed by a team of 125 engineers who keep the information up-to-date and streamlined and are available 24/7. InTouch provides solutions and advice to Schlumberger's 52,000 employees in over 1,000 distinct locations in more than 80 countries, and its mobile service units operate 24/7 on drilling rigs. Schlumberger estimates that the InTouch portal has generated more than $200 million in cost savings and led to a 75 percent reduction in time necessary to make modifications. These are introspective VTCs too, even though they may be virtual.[9]

Other forms of everyday introspection include midyear pulse checks, sometimes done by a third party to ensure that all voices are heard; weekly team huddles or planning meetings; and town halls not just with CEOs but within teams. Introspection could include not only conducting but really listening to and leveraging exit interviews, which are a huge source of typically untapped knowledge and potential learning in most organizations.

Everyday introspection might also include simple questions that enable us to leverage positive momentum, such as *What is working well and why?* Similarly, *What is* not *working well and why?* can open the door to a flood of insights, particularly if many different stakeholder views are included, from frontline employees and managers to customers and suppliers. Critical to the effectiveness of these conversations is digging for underlying root causes so that we change or amplify the right things and not just treat surface-level symptoms. These types of introspections are wonderful opportunities for multistakeholder engagement and developing a shared understanding of challenges, which is essential for moving forward effectively.

An annual retreat might also be an element in an organization's portfolio of introspective activities. What is key and often missing in many organizations is the integration of retreat activities with other forms of introspection and follow-through. It should be clear that it is not a one-off. Meeting off-site can be effective for opening people's minds, building connectedness, and engaging in some recreational activities that facilitate both bonding and breakthrough thinking.

Introspective conversations often uncover failures, and it is important to distinguish between different types. There is *blameworthy failure,* such as AOL's paying $850 million for Bebo in 2008, which it sold in 2010 for $10 million. There is also *preventable* or *repeated failure,* which is costly. But *smart failure,* as Amy Edmonson of Harvard calls it, entails learning from and not repeating specific failures.[10] We may even want to build in rapid prototypes, trials, milestones, and a plan for disengagement so that we become more disciplined about smart failure. Here again, as leaders we need to create the space for success and failure to be reflected on, shared, discussed, and learned from.

Capitalizing on the unexpected is another aspect of embedding introspection into everyday processes, whether it is taking time to notice the white spot on your sneaker that led to Scotchgard or the now-famous temporary glue that led to the invention of Post-it notes, one of 3M's biggest grand slams. Other examples of unexpected innovations include Viagra, which was heart medicine that increased blood flow to (*ahem*) other places, as well as Novocain, which started as an ineffective anesthesia but was subsequently used as a numbing agent in dental work and other medical procedures. Each of these innovations required not only a discovery but a series of conversations that enabled the "failure" to be recast as a success.

As professional basketball star Michael Jordan famously said, "I've missed more than 9,000 shots in my career. I've lost almost 300 games. Twenty-six times I've been trusted to take the game-winning shot and missed." Just think about how that feels. But, as he notes, "I've failed over and over and over again in my life. And that is why I succeed."[11] He reflected on every single one of those missed shots and probably learned as much, if not more, from them than from some of his most spectacular shots. We also like to think that he shared some of those learnings and insights with his teammates in conversations that led to better results in subsequent games.

So, another aspect of introspection is fostering the ability to look hard at ourselves and our actions and choices from the outside in. Then we need to leave ego and sunk costs at the door and work with those around us to make the best this-day-forward decisions.

Finally, in organizations we often fail to take the time to think about and reflect on what should be stopped. We keep adding and building. Streamlining and simplifying usually occurs only when prompted by some sort of process. We need to include asking questions and having conversations about what we should stop, unlearn, and no longer do.

We can build in everyday introspection by integrating pre- and postmortems into every project plan, taking time for appreciations, and learning from what is working and not working as well as from failures. The key message is to take time for stillness and soulful reflection on what we are doing or about to do, consider its impact, and then develop awareness of what is really happening around us by sharing, listening, and conversing with those who can help us process what we are experiencing and provide us with insight. Pause often, breathe, and listen—whether it's five minutes of sharing ideas for improvement at the end of a meeting, a weeklong retreat, a chat with a client or customer, noticing what other organizations are doing, or noting macro trends on the horizon.

Outward Introspection

There is a classic corporate legend of the boiled frog: two Bunsen burners, two frogs, and a sixth-grade science class. The experiment supposedly goes as follows. Put a frog in the first pot of hot water being heated up, and not surprisingly the frog will jump out. Indeed, a vice president at Boston Consulting Group and a research associate from the Massachusetts Institute of Technology tested this for *Fast Company,* and on average the frogs jump out in 1.6 seconds with a leap of 57 centimeters. But if a frog is put into cold water and the heat is turned on, the frog supposedly will not notice that it is getting slowly boiled alive. In actuality, as *Fast Company* discovered, the frog in the initially cold water will save itself, on average in 4.2 seconds with a jump of 24 centimeters.[12]

The point of the story is that we often forget to pay attention to what is happening around us. We may be slowly adjusting to challenges and changes in context and not really seeing the big picture and the hot water we are in and how deadly it might be.

To avoid becoming a boiled frog, we need to be outwardly introspective and pay attention to our immediate context as well as what is happening outside the organization. We need to stay in touch with the external trends that affect us, know how to differentiate ourselves and position our company for ongoing success, and create needed value. We need to pay attention to macro forces such as environmental, economic, social, political, and ecological trends as well as to competitors and those on the periphery.

Fast-food, soda, and tobacco companies are good examples of boiling frogs. Trends in health do not happen disruptively but rather slowly over time. There is a growing shift away from fat and salt, water is replacing soda, and fewer kids are getting hooked on cigarettes. That is excellent news for our overall societal health, but it does pose challenges for companies in those industries.

Macro trends and forces such as these sometimes emerge gradually, like the slowly heating water. If companies are not paying attention or are in denial, they can get blindsided—or boiled, so to speak. Some companies figure out how to respond and reemerge stronger, but that is difficult to do. It entails ongoing outward introspection about macro trends and also keenly observing competitors. By noticing and learning best and next practices from our rivals, we can learn from their mistakes, avoid reinventing the wheel, and sidestep hazards.

We can also learn from companies doing analogous activities on the periphery. For example, understanding outsourcing banking processing for major financial services firms might offer insights to an entrepreneur building a back-end photo conversion–to–digital archiving business. Though they are in fundamentally different industries, both are outsourcing processes for large blue-chip companies.

Outward introspection also includes tracking and discussing the organization's impact, both positive and negative, on its stakeholders, whether its employees or the planet. Sometimes we need to go to 30,000 feet to get that big-picture, long-term view. Al Gore raised awareness of man's devastating impact on the planet, another boiling frog, with *An Inconvenient Truth*. We need to pay attention to our company's inconvenient truths, both how they look from 30,000 feet as well as from on the ground, and listen and learn from what our front-line employees and customers feel and think about our organization.

One example of a company that has been particularly amazing at outward introspection between that 30,000-foot futuristic, anticipatory view and the on-the-ground customer view is Apple.[13] Among its most renowned innovations are the iMac, iPod, iPhone, and iPad. With each of these revolutions, Apple pulled together and combined existing elements of its business in new and exciting ways.

For example, the iMac, which came on the market in 1998, was simple, with no cumbersome wiring, and aesthetically appealing, with a rainbow of color options. These two traits had not been previously incorporated into personal computers. Steve Jobs said at the time, "You can't just ask customers what they want and then try to give that to them. By the time you get it built, they'll want something new."[14] From the iMac to the next big Apple megahit—the iPod—this proved true.

In 2001 Apple introduced the iPod. Portable music players, such as the Sony Walkman and later the MP3 player, already existed. Apple's brilliance was in connecting the dots between accessing, owning, and listening to music—all while on the go. In 2007 Apple introduced an amazing product that combined a phone, computer, music player, calculator, camera, photo album, notepad, maps, and a global positioning system (and, later, apps): the iPhone. The iPhone and its many iterations were followed later by the iPad, another breakthrough product.

Time and again Apple combined its external insights, technology, and learnings with clever imagination to create products that are functional and playful and that users come to see as indispensable. In Jobs's words, "I think we're having fun. I think our customers really like our products. And we're always trying to do better."[15] The most brilliant strategists and visionaries, like Jobs, are continuously outwardly introspective and always one step ahead of the curve.

As part of doing outward introspection more effectively with their customers, some companies are moving away from market surveys. When was the last time you really took time to fill one out, and what happens to all that data anyway? Companies are finding that deep anthropological dives with consumers, lasting a day or even a week—where they learn how consumers use their products or identify their untapped needs as they talk with their customers face-to-face on their own turf—provide much richer and more valuable information. Anthropological dives enable rich insights and understanding about the real touchpoints of the product or service and how customers experience it.

A good example of truly understanding customer touchpoints is Specialized Bicycle Components, a company that found a solution to the common problem of impotence in male cyclists by redesigning its bike seats. You may recall one of its taglines: *Be able to raise more than your arms after the race.* Another example is Arm & Hammer, which figured out—through customer feedback—that baking soda was used less and less as a leavening agent in cooking and more as a tooth whitener, kitchen cleaner, odor reducer, and air freshener. Subsequently, Arm & Hammer was able to adjust and take advantage of consumer demand for baking soda for a variety of uses.

Another innovative example of outward introspection in action is one of the practices of Best Buy, an American multinational consumer electronics corporation. Best Buy created Twelpforce, which stands for *real-time technology help.* This online portal connects and supports customers struggling with learning and using electronic product features. Any customer can post a question, and within seconds employees in stores anywhere in the world race to respond. These virtual conversations also provide the organization with ongoing direct feedback about what customers are finding frustrating or difficult to understand with the company's products.

Thus, by being outwardly introspective and talking with our stakeholders, we can better ensure that we do not become boiling frogs that are overlooking key forces and patterns that may disrupt our industries. Outward introspection helps organizations understand how to differentiate themselves and uncover and discover seeds of future breakthrough successes. We might suddenly see, for example, how packaging used for medical supplies is also useful for packaging juice or that aspirin is a highly effective blood thinner.

Introspection as an Ongoing Journey

At this point it should be clear that introspection is an ongoing process. It includes a portfolio of activities, from monitoring our external context to exploring ourselves; bringing our experiences, narratives, and expectations to the fore; revisiting and rethinking; running experiments and pilots before launching new endeavors; and taking time to reflect after completing initiatives and projects. To create high-performing organizations, we need to continuously look both inward and outward when we are successful and equally so when we are in trouble.

When we succeed we often gloss over introspection, thinking it won't be that valuable; but introspection can help uncover the things that are working well that often go unnoticed because they are running smoothly. From that insight we can think about how to amplify or diffuse those capabilities and learnings more broadly. It can also help us avoid the trap of "success breeds failure," when we get swept up in our triumphs and cover up, ignore, or fail to notice our faults and shortcomings.

Introspection is particularly critical when things are not going well. Often we are so panicked and filled with fear that we just shut down the contemplative side of our brains, but under difficult conditions is exactly when we should *not* go silent and withdraw. We need to talk, analyze, and figure it out. We need to be inwardly introspective to uncover what is not working well and get to the reasons why so that we can improve.

One way to gain some insight on the good, the bad, and the ugly is to surround ourselves with people who give us that outside-in perspective. Introspection alone is helpful, but we need a sounding board—the right people to bounce ideas off of and give honest feedback. Embedding introspection into our everyday lives and gaining the most insights and richness from our efforts requires the cultivation of an array of people who allow us to see ourselves and our actions and choices in new ways.

In their new book *Life Reimagined,* Richard Leider, best-selling author of *Re-packing Your Bags,* and Alan Webber, co-founder of *Fast Company,* talk about the need for sounding boards for individuals to function optimally. The same is true for us in organizations. We need to have conversations with those who hold a mirror to our actions and help us see ourselves as others do. We need those who give us the courage to experiment outside our comfort zones. We also need those who catalyze our thinking as well as those who focus on the details, those who help us see the big picture, and those who give us energy and support.[16]

We all make mistakes in life, and that is true of organizations as well. Most organizations take detours or derail now and then. It is unrealistic to try to create an infallible company, with thousands of employees and stakeholders who are faultless. The real question is, *How do we respond when things go off kilter?* When the going gets tough, what do we do? What we learn from exceptional companies is that crises become pivotal moments in the life of the organization. If we acknowledge our challenges and collectively dialogue and work together to meet those obstacles, such pivotal moments can inspire rather than disengage stakeholders.

At the heart of introspection is the ability to ask questions and find answers free from filters of fear and doubt and others' expectations.

We need that beginner's mind and the ability to be curious and explore, to not let the past cloud our view, and to be authentic rather than try to be what others expect. We need to be empty of expectations and see what might emerge.

So many people ignore ugly truths as if they would go away. They usually don't—they fester and get worse. But truths are actually great triggers for change. Acknowledging ugly truths enables us to become more open to discussing the elephants in the room and doing something about them. IBM did this in a big way when it created the first Values Jam, and 319,000 global employees weighed in. The company opened up a conversation about the gap between the talk (what their values were) and the walk (how they lived them). This virtual dialogue, which started by inviting everyone's input over 72 hours, led to a redefinition of IBM's top three values:

- Dedication to every client's success

- Innovation that matters, for our company and for the world

- Trust and personal responsibility in all relationships[17]

What started as a festering crisis was transformed through collective introspection into ownership, unity, and strength.

Interestingly, IBM also launched a Values Jam business for other companies, which offered the same type of internal introspection through crowdsourcing. For example, after being fined $450 million for a rate-fixing scandal, Barclays used a Values Jam facilitated by IBM to have necessary conversations around realigning and recommitting to its values. The event engaged 140,000 employees through 16 forums around five key values: respect, integrity, service, excellence, and stewardship. Each participant discussed, shared, and collaborated with others around two questions: *What do these values mean to me?* and *How will we live them?*"[18]

Barclays crowdsourced internally, but another key stakeholder is customers. The My Starbucks Idea program is a great example of customer crowdsourcing. Launched in 2008 by Starbucks, the website has gathered more than 130,000 customer-generated ideas.[19] Suggestions from customers range from product ideas, such as the Pumpkin Spice Latte and the Toasted Marshmallow Creme Frappuccino. They also include Starbucks's experience-enhancing ideas, such as "splash sticks" that prevent the beverage from spilling through the lid opening. Other ideas included free Wi-Fi for anyone sitting in the store and mobile payment through drive-thrus, where one can pay using a smartphone. More recently, a crowdsourced idea helped Starbucks launch its card mobile app.

Involvement ideas range from free coffee for people who vote in a local election to a request for Starbucks to become more mindful of issues in its supply chain, such as helping uncover the etiology of coffee plant diseases that are shutting down Central American growers. Starbucks gathers ideas by reaching out and listening to customers; but more importantly, these ideas become springboards for reflections on current practices and processes, and they trigger discussions that otherwise would not have occurred.

Free The Children (FTC) is another organization that excels in its openness to continuous introspection, which has helped it carve a new path in international development. The conventional approach to international development when FTC started was soliciting donations door to door and through telemarketing. Then these NGOs (nongovernmental organizations) would set up in crisis locations that were receiving news coverage because the media exposure helped the organization raise more money for its cause. Most of these international development NGOs typically competed against one another for scarce funds and needed to deduct administrative expenses from donations to keep their organizations afloat.

The FTC team turned this model on its head, morphing as they went. Introspective from the start and open to wherever the journey might lead, founder Craig Kielburger did not follow the approach of other international development organizations. He was 12 when he founded FTC, and although he was told that he needed adults to do the work, he challenged that assertion. A kid himself at the time, he knew that children could make a difference. They have a voice and an ability to mobilize others. Today FTC's core values say it all:

Commitment and passion

- We thinking and we acting

- Getting the job done…period

- Humility, gratitude, and appreciation in all endeavours

- Honoring every stakeholder

- Empowering youth to change the world

- Shameless idealism[20]

Kids are the heart of the organization. Whether they are running bake sales locally, gathering spare pennies in Canada to raise $7 million in a campaign called Change for Change, or building schools in emerging countries, FTC lives its values. Not only did Craig shift the engine of the organization from adults to kids but he and his brother, Marc, also continuously transformed FTC's business model.

Craig started by creating rescue houses for kids. Then he realized that children would stay only temporarily, going back to their villages to help out at home. Craig and Marc then shifted the focus to schools and education. That worked until they realized that girls with household responsibilities, such as carrying water, were unable to attend, so they morphed again. In their next reinvention, they created five pillars of sustainable development—education; clean water and sanitation; health; alternative income and livelihood; and agriculture and food security—with the goal of the village's never needing charity again. Rather than impose Western solutions, they "drink tea" with local villages to learn what their needs are and they collaborate with locals to build independence and sustainable success.[21]

Breaking with tradition in international development yet again, Craig and Marc then developed a sister organization to Free The Children called Me to We. Me to We's vision is to provide people with "better choices for a better world, including socially conscious and environmentally friendly clothes and accessories, as well as life-changing international volunteer trips, leadership training programs and materials, an inspirational speakers' bureau, and books that address issues of positive social change."[22] Half of Me to We's net profit goes to FTC, so no administrative costs are deducted from donations that FTC receives.

Recently, rather than compete with other NGOs, FTC used its annual celebratory We Day, where thousands of youth join to celebrate and reflect on their make-a-difference contributions, to further break with conventional approaches. We Day is an inspirational event blending pop concerts and launch events for the year's educational initiatives; it features celebrities and political figures from around the world, sharing conversations and sparking initiatives with FTC's activist youth.[23] Now in 11 cities across North America and the United Kingdom, these events are platforms not only for FTC but for any social cause. Craig and Marc are building partnerships and bridges across NGOs, propelling positive change and addressing the world's most pressing issues.

Thus, with openness to continuous introspection on their journeys of evolution, companies like FTC transform again and again. Despite the skeptics, FTC proved that kids can make a difference, that they can build a business model that enables all donations to go to the cause, that an NGO can be collaborative in building partnerships with other NGOs and succeed, and that each individual's energy and passion when pooled collectively can powerfully and positively transform the world.

Conclusion

Introspective VTC leads to insights that change our actions and decisions. Sometimes such introspective conversations prevent us from making decisions we might regret later. Sometimes they enable us to learn from what goes well and not so well and chart our actions to amplify successes and learn from and address challenges. Sometimes they wake us up to the context in which we are immersed so that we don't become boiled frogs. Introspection also prevents us from overreacting based on past experiences and events that are unrelated to current circumstances.

As we engage in introspection, we need to try to step away from ego, pride, and embarrassment and instead ask questions and listen to the voices around us, trying to see things as others do. The effort might include embedding introspection into everyday processes—such as after-action reviews, pre- and postmortems, and appreciations—as well as conducting outward introspections. We must realize that introspection is an ongoing journey. Introspective values also urge us to reflect on the type of inquiries and research we conduct and how we view our connections and contributions to the world at large. Finally, introspection asks us to ask questions about the questions we ask.

CONVERSATION STARTERS FOR INTROSPECTIVE VALUES

Bridging the values gap through self- and collective reflection on how everyday decisions and actions facilitate or impede living our values successfully

- Are we achieving what we hoped for?
- What are our values? How do we live those values within the organization? Are they working for us?
- What is working well and why? How can we amplify those successes?
- What is not working well and why? How can we learn and improve?
- How much time do we spend on our priorities?
- What inquiries should we conduct? What research is useful in helping us reach our goals?
- What questions should we ask ourselves?
- What actions and habits do we take for granted?
- What narratives underlie what we do? How does our language affect our ideas, actions, habits, and values?
- What should we stop doing? What should we unlearn?
- What does a view from 30,000 feet tell us? What does a view from the ground tell us?
- Do we check for biases when we make decisions?
- Do we do pre-mortems and after-action reviews?
- Do we reflect individually first and then share with the team to capture everyone's viewpoint?
- Do we collectively reflect?
- What is essential and gives us meaning and energy?
- Who is silenced in our conversations?
- What are the elephants in the room—the things that are not discussed?
- What policies and practices help us embed introspection on an ongoing basis?

CHAPTER 6

Historical Values: Exploring the Impact of Our Past

Every person has a history. As French philosopher and author Albert Camus purportedly once said, "Life is a sum of all your choices." Each of our histories is uniquely us. These histories become encapsulated as memories that follow a story line, although over time the story line may evolve. Our story lines also dramatically influence and shape the upcoming choices we make and actions we take.

The same is true for organizations. Every organization is the sum of all the choices and decisions of everyone in it. This history shapes the organization's collective memory and identity—how those in the organization view the world and their past, current, and future choices and actions. History is woven into the fabric of the organization. Sometimes it is widely celebrated and pondered; other times it is so embedded that it goes unnoticed. But without history we do not really understand how we came to be who we are as individuals or as a collective organization.

The Role of History in Values through Conversation

The reason we teach history to kids in school is so that they can understand the struggles, challenges, decisions, and paths that led to the life

AT A GLANCE: HISTORICAL VALUES

Bridging the values gap by exploring how our past choices led to who we are today and shape who we could be in the future

Benefits

- Create a collective identity
- Uncover our roots and evolution
- Raise awareness about differing accounts of history
- Reveal assumptions
- Enable more-informed choices for the future
- Refresh and energize while preserving legacy and continuity

Principles

- Gratitude for the journey
- Creating collective history and narratives
- Honoring legacy while embracing evolution

Practices

- Capture history and choices
- Embed different voices to generate history
- Affirm collective identity
- Share stories
- Celebrate accomplishments and milestones
- Develop rituals and symbols
- Balance continuity and evolution

---

they enjoy today. Freedom for North American kids may be taken for granted until they learn how generations before them fought for freedom of speech, freedom of religion, freedom of the press, the right to vote and own land, and so much more. Purpose evolves over time, but without keeping history alive it may evolve to a place where it is hard to recognize by organizational leaders as well as other stakeholders to whom it is so crucial.

Many companies operate ahistorically, focusing their efforts on the present and the future with little regard for the past. They may give a nod to the occasional mention of a founder's name or use history to justify recommendations to maintain the status quo, but they tend to view history as an option that can be trash-talked or ignored. This type of approach assumes that the organization and the people within it can be removed from their context and their histories. It also downplays the demoralizing effect that erasing history has on those who spent years writing those historical chapters.

An ahistorical understanding sometimes arises in entrepreneurial firms that outlive their founders and go public. The purpose and values on which the company was built are often forgotten as it grows larger, becoming less than it could be. Each division may have some sense of the original mission, but the company as a whole may seem purposeless other than making a specific number for Wall Street.

Some companies go further and take an uncritical approach to their history, sometimes developing a very stylized version of it that often omits unsavory events in the past. With an unreflective view of their own history, it is difficult for such organizations to take seriously the idea of reflecting on current values.

The Benefits of History

Historical values focus on how to refresh and reenergize while preserving legacy and continuity. They help us retain the balance between an openness to revitalization and the enduring traditions, strategies, and practices of the past. Understanding the present with knowledge of history is enlightening. Now is a much more interesting place to be if we have some sense of how we got here. We cannot dive into a current problem and make much progress without a sense of history. To understand the roots of what is and is not working well and move forward, we need to know how things got started, what was happening externally and competitively, the stage of growth of the organization, the thinking at the time, and the evolution of the various factors at play.

There are always varying accounts of history from different vantage points. Everyone has his or her own particular version of the story and what the reality was at the time. It is essential to share those narratives to gain a more complete view of history. Discussing the differences among the narratives is extremely important for bringing values conversation to life.

Recall those boiling-frog companies in chapter 5. One of those firms made products that customers wanted but that could also be harmful to their health. For many years the company simply denied that its products had unhealthy side effects. Under constant pressure from external stakeholders, the company finally acknowledged those health impacts (in part because it was forced to do so) and began devoting resources to countering the negative effects. Until leaders in the company confronted their own history, they simply could not move forward—and telling themselves a story that everyone knew to be untrue was an ineffective way of dealing with history.

History also evolves as certain aspects become ritualized and immortalized and as new voices offer divergent perspectives on what we thought we knew. Gen Z—those kids born after 1995—grew up with digital technology. While baby boomers are lamenting the impact of technology on society, these kids are spending 10 hours a day in right-brain, fast-twitch activity. Their view of the history of current times would probably be written differently than that of a boomer. Only by hearing and spinning together multiple voices can we gain a robust picture of the times.

With these examples we see how we can narrow the values gap by having conversations that enable us to create shared histories. And by working through multiple perspectives on the same phenomenon, including how our interpretations and narratives of organizational history converge and differ, we can open up a dialogue on how our history shapes the values, routines, and structures we have today. It might trigger analysis on how past choices can both blind us and open up new possibilities. It might include asking what processes can help improve the understanding of organizational history on an ongoing basis.

At a minimum, conversations about our past enable us to uncover the convergence of our history and where we are now that is essential for forming a collective identity and moving forward together. History helps us understand where we are and have been, and it offers insights on where we might go and how to get there. It helps us see what makes us distinctive. We make smarter decisions when we know the successes and failures of the past and have learned from them. Historical inquiry moves beyond recording history to questioning and analyzing it and thinking about how the organization might do things differently in the future—how to transform past history into future positive growth.

VTC Principles and Practices: Bridging the Values Gap by Bringing Historical Values to Life

One company that consistently met Wall Street earnings estimates was composed of a number of good businesses that had been assembled by M&As in industries that were only marginally related to one another. The company was doing well, but it had not had a breakthrough product in some time. It ran as a conglomerate, meeting expectations and making incremental progress. Its younger executives thought that the company could be more than its numbers and the sum of its parts. In fact, each of the divisions had come from a legacy of pioneers, founders who had been in the forefront of creating their industries. A number of these young executives were hungry to find the commonalities among the pioneers in terms of their values. They urged the CEO to undertake such an effort, believing that they could energize the company to perform far beyond Wall Street estimates and solve a morale problem that could only be described as malaise.

Unfortunately, the CEO was unable to look past the numbers. He appreciated the history of the divisions but saw little need to build on it. Under pressure from the young executives, he did make a half-hearted attempt to set forth some companywide values. Everyone knew that all he really cared about were the numbers, however, so the values conversation was bogged down. It could have begun by celebrating the company's history and showing how the pioneering spirit that was once in all the divisions could be reenergized. The company continues to perform well, but there is still an internal feeling that it could be more than it is.

In times of crisis, history helps us see what led to earlier successes that might inform the present even if the context has changed. When we are drifting away from what we are good at, understanding history helps us get back on course. VTC about history might include choosing to create a big fiftieth-anniversary celebration at Lamborghini, which we talk more about later in this chapter, or it might be as simple as deciding to take funny photos while kayaking at a Microsoft retreat in Lake Muskoka country.

Understanding history can help us respect and honor the legacy of our organizations, understand our uniqueness, share our perspectives, and build insight for evolution and future growth. It helps ensure that we see the bridges between past choices and future actions.

Bringing history to life looks different in every company, but there are some principles that underpin historical aspects of VTC in thriving organizations.

Gratitude for the Journey

Taking our history seriously involves understanding our roots and the chapters of our life stories. As humans we have both DNA—the genetic instructions we inherit from our parents that govern how our bodies develop and function—and also emotional roots and choices, the experiences and decisions that shape how our lives unfold. Part of VTC about history involves making us aware of what is embedded in our organizational etiology: What are the roots of our organization? How was the company started? How do our roots and early struggles, challenges, choices, and learnings affect who we are now?

For example, maybe our organizational structure is some wacky combination of function, product, and matrix. That likely is a historical artifact of political battles won and lost, capabilities and interests of past leaders, and what was happening in the market when some team was rethinking structure or maybe a new CEO was trying to leave his or her mark. History also stems from the context outside the organization, including that of the industry, region, country, and, of course, those with whom we work. As individuals we have a personal history that is interwoven with that of our family, friends, work, community, and region. Similarly, organizational trajectories are a reflection of every choice, chapter, and context that influenced the organization's evolution into what it is today.

Just as every challenge and hurdle tests but also strengthens us in different ways as individuals, the same is true for organizations. Surviving and choosing how to navigate through rough waters allows us to see the stamina and vigor with which we can overcome difficulties.

Take, for example, Mayor Rudy Giuliani's encouraging the citizens of New York and the United States to consider their history and draw strength from it after the 9/11 terrorist attack on the World Trade Center in Manhattan: "The attacks of September 11 were intended to break our spirit. Instead we have emerged stronger and more unified. We feel renewed devotion to the principles of political, economic, and religious freedom, the rule of law and respect for human life. We are more determined than ever to live our lives in freedom."[1] Embracing a historical perspective, Giuliani became the face of New York during the crisis, channeling shock and confusion into hope and resiliency.

People everywhere responded and joined together to help in the aftermath and recovery. Stories were shared, memories were captured, and memorials were created.

Coming to a place where we can find the positive aspects and see the skills that emerged from the challenges we have faced often means we are better prepared for future struggles. We have developed the ability not to wallow in our failures but rather learn from them and realize how we are better as a result. It is about reflecting on our scars and celebrating them for what they have taught us and how far we have come. They give us our distinctive skills, capabilities, and mind-set. Similarly, in organizations we need to understand our decisions and actions, whether brilliant or misguided, as embedded in the context and mind-set of the time and ask ourselves what insights they offer.

Sometimes we explicitly choose to recognize struggles and successes. Other times our triumphs and achievements go unnoticed and uncelebrated. Focusing on history and having conversations helps bring these accomplishments to the fore. They allow us to discuss and build a shared understanding of what happened and why. In this process we need to hear and embrace differing views. Just as the history of the United States has been challenged and revised by women, African Americans, indigenous Americans, and other historically disenfranchised groups, our organizational histories need to capture and nurture multiple and often fringe voices.

A historical view also enables us to see patterns and cycles. In a tornado of events and the onslaught of never-ending information, sharing our views of the past and collectively building our history helps us pull the bits and pieces of what has happened and is happening into a story line that helps us and those around us make sense of the past and the present. Taking time to have conversations about our history and our differing interpretations of past events enables us to create the collective history and narratives so essential for a strong, shared identity.

Creating a Collective History and Narratives

As William McNeill, a well-known professor emeritus of history at the University of Chicago, aptly notes, "Historical knowledge is no more and no less than carefully and critically constructed collective memory."[2]

Just as we each have memories that capture our personal history, organizations need collective memories. In organizations we need to consciously cultivate and share our stories to preserve our history and construct a collective memory just as we do as individuals, consciously sharing history with our kids and those around us.

One of the best ways to engage stakeholders around history is through storytelling. Stories engage us and win our hearts and minds. Understanding and sharing the organization's history is vital for inspiring us and ensuring that the founding story stays alive. In chapter 5 we discussed how Free The Children leverages introspection to create breakthrough business models, but we have not yet shared how FTC started and how it promulgates story throughout the organization to foster passion and engagement.

Free The Children began when 12-year-old Craig Kielburger was searching for comics in the *Toronto Star* at breakfast one morning and saw a story about a boy his same age who was born in South Asia. This boy, Iqbal Masih, was forced into slavery at the age of four when his parents borrowed money from a carpet factory owner for their eldest son's wedding. Iqbal worked 12 hours a day, seven days a week. He and other children were tortured, beaten, and hung upside down by ropes in a back room if they fell behind. Iqbal knew he would remain a slave forever because once a child slave, your debts could never be paid off; in fact, the debt grew as Iqbal's family was charged for the one small daily bowl of rice he ate. With the help of a human rights organization, Iqbal started school and soon became an eloquent spokesperson for children's rights. He was shot to death while riding a bicycle to see his uncle. His voice of freedom was silenced, but, as another child slave declared, "A thousand new Iqbals were born."[3] One of those was Craig Kielburger.

In his seventh-grade class that day, Kielburger read Iqbal's story aloud, then asked his friends to help him do something about children's rights. The movement of empowering children to help other children began with a question, a conversation starter. Now, two decades later, what began as a garage initiative by a 12-year-old to free children from poverty, exploitation, and the notion that they are powerless to effect change has engaged more than 2 million youth. FTC has contributed 15 million volunteer hours to better things locally and globally; built more than 650 schools in Asia, Africa, and Latin America; shipped $16 million worth of medical supplies to 40 countries; and enabled the delivery of clean water, healthcare, and sanitation to 1.2 million people.

Free The Children actively shares this founding story to inspire people both inside and outside the organization. School groups learn and share the story. It is featured on FTC's website and is the backbone of its annual We Day celebrations, where thousands of children who have earned their way to attend through community and school involvement join together and retell that story; they also build new stories of conquering challenges and generating positive change. The celebration includes young celebrities such as Demi Lovato, Selena Gomez, and the Jonas Brothers. The essence of We Day centers on hearing and celebrating inspirational stories and histories of challenges and social triumphs. It features such performers as Mia Farrow, Martin Sheen, Nelly Furtado, K'naan, and Natalie Portman; athletes Magic Johnson and Laila Ali; political activists Martin Luther King III, Jane Goodall, Al Gore, Mikhail Gorbachev, and former national chief Shawn A-in-chut Atleo of the Assembly of First Nations; as well as local youth and emerging grassroots leaders.

Free The Children understands that this founding story energizes, inspires, and gives hope to all of its stakeholders—yet it mobilizes volunteers through more than the founding story. Stakeholder passions are also ignited by the new stories shared at every We Day, in participating schools, and through social media. By sharing their founding story as one example of what is possible, those involved with FTC transform into change activists and propel this incredible youth movement that continues to grow exponentially. Clearly, FTC has thought carefully about how to foster "living history" through stories both old and new.[4]

For other organizations, narrowing the values gap and building historical VTC might involve grand celebrations of the company's journey. Lamborghini, the luxury car maker that names cars after famous bulls and whose car designs are inspired by insects and fighter planes, sells cars that cost from $400,000 to $4 million. The company builds each car by hand, proudly upholding an Italian heritage and tradition and "marrying the science of engineering with the 'art of irrational romance.'" The company recently celebrated its fiftieth anniversary. In 2013, to mark what it called "100 years of innovation in half the time," Lamborghini organized the largest gathering of its cars ever for a six-day, 750-mile drive through Italy.[5]

Owners of nearly 350 cars from 27 countries gathered in Milan for the Grande Giro, or Grand Tour. After stops in Rome, Pisa, and Bologna, they made their way to Sant'Agata Bolognese, the home of Lamborghini, where prizes were given for the most impressive rides. The world saw the reveal of the most outrageous Lamborghini ever—the Veneno—which goes from 0 to 100 in 2.3 seconds and costs $3.9 million. Only three Venenos were made, and they were snapped up immediately. An amazing display of fireworks wrapped up this historical celebration that was featured in the news, attracted new buyers, and generated lots of social media hits.

The event was significant for Lamborghini, a historical opportunity to celebrate decades of hard work and the successes that emerged both within the company and with its customers. Indeed, sometimes bringing back popular nostalgic products opens up new markets, whether it's the Volkswagen Beetle or the Ford Mustang. But honoring history is much more than that. For Lamborghini this celebration was an opportunity to foster and share collective pride in the company and its heritage.

History might also include rituals and symbols. Honda in Japan pioneered morning exercises as part of the daily routine for newly hired assembly line employees, establishing a ritual with both tangible and intangible benefits. Universities have convocations, school colors, annual homecomings, and orientation rituals. The offices of international design and consulting firm IDEO have an open layout, with employees free to decorate their spaces with creativity-inducing artifacts. Nike has the swoosh, which symbolizes speed.

Onboarding in many companies is another form of history sharing. It might be sending associates to Disney University to learn about founder Walt Disney and all the famous characters. Disney also has a separate physical location for customers and other stakeholders that honors Walt Disney and reinforces the company's founding story, the timeline of its development, and its key values.

It might be a four-week custom-developed company values program at Zappos, where managers dig deeply, through numerous conversations, to ensure that new employees are a good cultural fit. As Zappos CEO Tony Hsieh says, "Many companies have core values, but they don't really commit to them. They usually sound more like something you'd read in a press release. Maybe you learn about them on day one of orientation, but after that it's just a meaningless plaque on the wall of the lobby."[6] So Zappos's orientation is different. Management shares the company history, the importance of customer service, the company's long-term vision, and the philosophy about company culture. Employees are then put on the phone for two weeks, taking calls and having conversations with customers, to really bring their *Deliver WOW through Service* number one value to life. This is how the company ensures that new employees understand Zappos's roots, what it stands for, and how it builds a shared history and understanding that at Zappos customer service truly permeates the entire company.

IKEA, Swedish manufacturer of do-it-yourself simplistic furniture sold internationally, has both an IKEA museum and an IKEA Together building to help keep the company's values and culture alive and thriving.

Building and cultivating history might also be as easy as Microsoft's taking photos during a retreat in the Lake Muskoka region and posting them to the company's virtual archives and intranet.

It could be the simple but powerful exercise of asking, "If we had to tell the story of our company, our division, our team, and our products, what might we want to include?" Engaging in such an exercise may reveal interesting insights about strategic and organizational choices and help bring historical values to life. It also helps bridge the values gap by facilitating discussions that reveal how values were upheld or undermined in the firm's past and how collective identity was fragmented or reinforced as a result. It might include asking what processes can help improve the understanding of an organization's past on an ongoing basis and how we transmit and share history as well as how we nurture multiple voices.

Thus, whether through story sharing, rituals, grand celebrations, or photos, sharing our collective narratives through conversations about our past is important for keeping history alive. Companies that invest in history and story sharing understand that creating convergence on history and where we are now is essential for cultivating a collective identity and the shared memory needed to be able to move forward together.

Honoring Legacy while Embracing Evolution

History is critical to each of us and to every organization, and it helps foster a deeper understanding of identity, collective memory, and shared journey. Yet we also need to find the delicate balance of what to preserve and what to let go. We want to cherish history, but we also need to evolve as our context changes or we move into new regions. These all become the next chapters of our organizational story, but lots of organizations have trouble finding that sweet spot of carrying history forward while adapting as needed.

Botched M&As such as the AOL–Time Warner merger and eBay's acquisition of Skype are classic examples. Indeed, according to a recent KPMG survey,[7] 83 percent of M&As fail to deliver value. Sometimes these failures are the result of bad project management, but M&As are notorious for stripping out history and destroying value largely because they don't conduct deep due diligence on what threads to bring forward as they strive to create a new entity. "Unexpected people issues" may be a euphemism in part for *We didn't understand the history and culture of each of the entities.*

A few companies do find a better balance. Kraft Foods, in its acquisition of Cadbury, is an example of a merger in which the leaders did carry forward the history of each company even as they merged. The joining of these two companies had a rocky start, but leaders from both sides took to heart the truth that "a sophisticated understanding of the past is one of the most powerful tools we have for shaping the future."[8] A new intranet branded Coming Together was introduced, and it was rife with relevant content highlighting the parallels and accomplishments of Kraft Foods and Cadbury, reinforcing the message that the merger was a natural fit, well thought out, and set up to succeed. People could blog about their thoughts and reactions.

Highlights included the fact that both companies had a history of valuing employees in the dawn of the twentieth century when other companies treated workers as commodities; there were also parallels in the biographies of the two founders, James L. Kraft and John Cadbury.[9] In short, sharing these histories with people in both companies—underscoring parallels about the companies' founders and historical paths—was deliberate, sensitive, and helpful in creating better conversations that ultimately paved the way for a smooth integration.

Moving into new geographical regions is another opportunity to honor legacy and adapt. Sometimes companies graft new local history in the process, as evident in the highly successful Tokyo Disneyland and, in contrast, the unsuccessful Disneyland Paris. When moving into new markets, every company, even those as successful as Disney, has to learn how to balance honoring the legacy and tradition that made the company great and adapting and tailoring that legacy to local culture and traditions.

After opening the first international Disney theme park in Tokyo, Japan, in 1983, Disney made minimal cultural adaptations to the Disney experience. For the Japanese the Magic Kingdom filled with Americana was something unusual and different that they wanted to experience. Mickey and Minnie Mouse, Donald Duck, Goofy, Cinderella, and classic attractions such as It's a Small World, Pirates of the Caribbean, and the Main Street Parade enchanted Japanese visitors.

Disney executives assumed when they opened Disneyland Paris in 1992 with the same American dream experience that it would be equally successful. They failed to explore their past and rethink how things might be different when they moved to Europe. As soon as guests arrived on opening day, however, they discovered the mistaken assumptions they had made.

They had overcompensated on some features of the Disney experience. For example, Disney executives had assumed that the French would want their typical breakfast of croissants and coffee but instead found 2,500 locals anxiously wanting an all-American breakfast with waffles, pancakes, eggs, and bacon. They also erred when they created full-service restaurants familiar to Europeans instead of the self-service types typical of Disney parks in the United States; the European guests wanted the latter.

Disney executives also failed to have conversations that would have shed light on vacation patterns in Europe. Disney expected that most of the Paris guests would be French; but because travel throughout the continent is easy and common, people came from across Europe, including Belgium, Germany, Spain, Switzerland, and Scandinavia. And not realizing that Europeans preferred walking (because they failed to explore this through conversations with the locals), Disney also built expensive trams to provide transportation around the park. Red nail polish on women and facial hair on men posed additional challenges to the dress code for Disney employees, creating tensions that again could have been explored through dialogue. And without checking with customers, Disney toned down the swag in its boutiques only to discover that Europeans actually wanted Mickey Mouse hats and other Disney memorabilia.

Culturally, there were lifestyle differences between Europeans and Americans that were overlooked, again because few conversations with key stakeholders occurred. Unlike Americans, many Europeans have a tradition of one long vacation during the summer instead of several short vacations throughout the year. These customs did not fit well with Disney, especially when paired with overpriced entrance fees and lodging prices that Europeans were used to paying only for luxury hotels in the city center. As in its American parks, Disney banned alcohol, not realizing that France is the world's biggest wine consumer and that most French have wine daily along with their lunch and dinner.

When Disney opened the doors to Disneyland Paris, anticipating 11 million visitors and $100 million profit, it instead lost $900 million within two years due to its failure to fine-tune the balance between legacy Disney and European adaptation.

With this example we see the cost of not engaging in conversations with customers before launching and the delicate balance of honoring Disney's legacy within the history of Europe and then embracing the evolution needed for success. French businessman

Philippe Bourguignon took over as president of the park in 1992. He changed the name from Euro Disney Resort to Disneyland Paris, and he talked with local customers about expectations and preferences. He lowered the entrance fee and hotel prices, changed the restaurant menus to cater to diverse European cultures, and saw that Disney characters spoke in a multitude of European languages. These were seemingly simple changes that made the difference between a flop and a success. In 2012 Disneyland Paris celebrated its twentieth anniversary with stellar results.[10]

A further example of how the company has evolved while honoring its legacy is the Disney princesses. Recall the early stories of Cinderella, Sleeping Beauty, and Snow White. Although there was some strength of character in the original stories, their commercialization created superficially obsessed, helpless girly-girl victims waiting to be kissed and rescued by a prince. Eventually, Disney caught on to how outdated these characterizations were.

It began with Pocahontas (1995), who refused to leave her people to accompany her lover to Europe. This was followed by Scottish princess and seasoned archer Merida in *Brave* (2012) and *Frozen*'s fearless, ever-optimistic Anna (2013), who battles Everest-like winter conditions to save her sister. These new age heroines are not only *not* waiting for a prince but are clever problem solvers who overcome numerous challenges to achieve their happy endings. What accounts for strong female characters? They are the result of customer analysis. But also note that movies like *Frozen,* the highest-grossing animated film of all time at $1.3 billion and the fifth-highest-grossing film of any sort, happened because more women were included in the conversation. Indeed, the *Frozen* screenplay was written by a woman, Jennifer Lee, who also co-directed the blockbuster movie.[11]

McDonald's executives have also initiated conversations with the company's stakeholders, particularly its customers. As a result, the franchise has flourished in *glocalization,* a sociological term it uses to talk about the bridge of globalization and localization in goods and services. With the variation of diets in Africa, Asia, North America, South America, Russia, and the Middle East, McDonald's has learned from customers in each region how to alter its menus to accommodate local preferences and dietary restrictions and have a positive impact on its bottom line.

For example, the McDonald's classic hamburger is offered in addition to the Teriyaki burger in Singapore, the kimchee burger in Korea, and the McVeggie burger in India. McDonald's has added green tea to the classic McFlurry flavors in Japan. In Muslim countries McDonald's offers a halal menu, including the McFalafel sandwich, Filet-O-Fish, and the McArabia Chicken (grilled chicken sandwich served on flatbread). During the Chinese New Year, McDonald's served meals with a horoscope of the 12 zodiac animals of Chinese astrology and the traditional red packets called *hongbao*. Through these alterations to the classic menu items and practices, McDonald's is able to expand into international markets and accommodate local food preferences and needs.[12]

As these examples show, we need to honor our organization's history and culture, but we also need to have conversations with our stakeholders as we move into new markets so that we know when and how to adapt the brand. That evolution might mean integrating unique local customs and updating or letting go of some traditional aspects.

Conclusion

Marketing legend Paul Alofs, now CEO of Princess Margaret Cancer Centre, the largest Canadian cancer facility and one of the top cancer treatment hospitals globally, notes that to truly capture a company's aspirations we must reflect on the past and find "unity, clarity, and inspiration."[13]

Organizations are idiosyncratic combinations of people and activities, intermeshed in ever-changing contexts that evolve in unique ways. History helps the people within a company understand the connections between where they have been and who they are now and why. Conversations around history provide insight into the key changes and choices the organization has made and how they shape what the company is and stands for today. Historical understanding also solidifies the organization's identity by encouraging different interpretations of the impact of past choices and their consequences for different stakeholder groups. Seeking to understand history gives us insight on the aspects of our legacy that should be preserved and those we need to let go of or adapt.

The historical part of VTC focuses on sharing our interpretations of the past and collectively creating an identity-shaping story line that we learn from and that guides our decisions moving forward. Thus, just as Camus noted for individuals, our organizations are the sum of our company's experience, which includes our successes, failures, challenges, and lessons learned.

CONVERSATION STARTERS FOR HISTORICAL VALUES

Bridging the values gap by exploring how our past choices led to who we are today and shape who we could be in the future

- How do our interpretations of our organization's history converge and differ? What do we learn from these different views of reality?
- How does our history shape the values, routines, structures, and processes we have today?
- How does our history blind us or open up possibilities?
- What can be learned from the choices, processes, and decisions that forged our historical path?
- Which of our processes help us understand our history on an ongoing basis?
- How do we share our history?
- How do we collect stories from today that will become our history for tomorrow?
- When and how should we have conversations that keep our history alive?
- Where and how do we capture our history?
- How do we create processes that enable us to nurture our history while also being open to when we need to let go and evolve?
- How often do we have celebrations connected to our history?
- How do we help newcomers to the organization learn about our history?

CHAPTER **7**

Connectedness Values: Creating a Sense of Belonging and Community

Something totally unexpected happened at 8:15 one Monday morning at Colgate University, a small liberal arts college in the northeastern United States. More than 300 students staged a sit-in at the university's admissions building to protest the treatment of minority students and the lack of inclusivity on campus. The problem had been simmering for some time, and the mood was angry and tense. The students publicized their efforts on social media, using the hashtag #CanYouHearUsNow and posting video testimonials. The news media picked up the story.

Instead of reacting defensively and calling security and the police or trying to shut down the protest, university president Jeffrey Herbst and other university leaders sat down with the students and listened to their stories:

> I listened to several dozen students speak in raw, emotional terms about greatly painful experiences that stemmed from issues of race and identity, as well as class, sexual orientation, and, for international students, national origin. They recounted occasions

AT A GLANCE: CONNECTEDNESS VALUES

Bridging the values gap through how we have conversations, interact, lead, follow, and work together to achieve our collective purpose and aspirations

Benefits

- Thriving, energizing workplace
- Problems are solved quickly and easily
- Innovation and creativity
- Whole is bigger than the sum of the parts
- Magnet for talent
- Customers love the company

Principles

- Better together
- Relational work is *real* work
- Being one's whole self

Practices

- Share, distribute, and decentralize ownership and decision rights
- Create the space for connectedness
- Devote time to and reward relationship and community building
- Enable with help and support
- Do "head, heart, and hands" check-ins
- Listen and use words that reinforce connection
- Cultivate trustful, respectful, open, and nurturing meeting practices
- Foster bringing our whole selves to work

of when they had been insulted on campus, felt marginalized both inside and outside of the classroom, and felt unsafe....

Many in the room were moved to tears by their heart-wrenching stories.[1]

This honest, open sharing of experiences set the stage for both sides to be willing to understand each other and find agreement. The student leaders presented the president with their demands in a non-threatening way, with a focus on "common ground." They stated how deeply they believed in Colgate's mission to be an inclusive learning institution and acknowledged that the problem is one of the most difficult faced by all institutions in the United States and globally. With achieving Colgate's mission as their goal, they listed concerns and action plans.

The administration showed its support for their efforts and positive approach to solving the problem. President Herbst condemned the racist incidents and expressed his and the university's solidarity with the students taking part in the protest: "Acts of racism and homophobia have no place at Colgate and will not be tolerated. Prejudice can devastate our community: it chills the campus climate, making members of our community feel unwelcome, shackles the mind with stereotypical thinking and bigotry, and keeps us from reaching our true potential as caring, intelligent people who are prepared to live in an increasingly global and diverse society....Together as a community, we can and must hold ourselves and each other to a higher standard."[2]

Both sides used inclusive language. The president referred to the event as a "peaceful demonstration." Both sides talked about common ground, shared goals, and the importance of working together. The sit-in lasted the week, with hours and hours of conversations and discussions. Together members of the administration and the Colgate University Association for Critical Collegians (ACC) formulated a 21-point roadmap for the future. On Friday the students, faculty, and

administration marched together to the chapel on campus in a celebration of the 100-hour-long demonstration.[3]

President Herbst concluded the week with the statement, "As a
liberal arts institution, we must do everything we can, together, to create an environment that is welcoming to all students, so that all can
freely explore diverse perspectives and worldviews." ACC founders
echoed those sentiments: "Colgate must fulfill its promise of being an
inclusive institution for students of all backgrounds. Our hope moving
forward is that this new action plan will create lasting change in our
campus community."[4] This story is a wonderful example of the power
of connectedness conversations and facing a shared issue through
listening, learning, and identifying common needs and solutions to
effect lasting change. The key principles the leaders employed—leading proactively, valuing everyone's input, and facilitating trust and
high accountability—enabled the conflict to be transformed into a
joint action plan to create a new and better future.

The Role of Connectedness in Values through Conversation

Connectedness values focus on how we converse and interact to
achieve our collective purpose and aspirations. We all know a connected organization when we see one in action. The place is thriving
and energizing, and the people are pumped up about what they are
doing. People are themselves and are being stretched to reach their
potential. They are passionate about their work and can count on one
another. Problems are solved quickly and creatively. New ideas bubble
up and are nurtured. People in the company say hello when they pass
each other instead of averting their eyes. When there is disagreement
in meetings, folks try to understand one another's point of view and
contributions. Customers love the company and come back again and
again, and they tell their friends to do the same. Suppliers work hard

to meet the collective expectations of others in the organization. The company is a magnet for the best talent. The place oozes excellence.

Connectedness values focus on our relationships with one another and how we converse and share ideas as we work together. This aspect of VTC captures how we lead and follow and our beliefs about effective processes and how to accomplish goals. The beauty of creating an organization with cohesiveness, cooperation, reciprocity, and belonging is that everyone brings out the best in one another.

Sometimes connectedness is missing because its importance is not even on top management's radar. Other times values statements may be well intended but there is a significant gap between the "talk" and the official view, and the "walk" or day-to-day reality of life. The company might assert that "Our employees are our most important asset," or words like *respect, empathy, care, inclusiveness, accountability,* and *growth* appear in its values statement. These are virtuous ideas that might make life in organizations better, but when actions are inconsistent and speak louder than words, the good intentions fall pretty flat.

Whether connectedness is never touched upon or the company talks connectedness but fails to demonstrate it, when connectedness values are missing, life at work feels empty. We have all worked in an organization where everyone is on autopilot, no one is happy, and work feels like solely a contractual arrangement. Leaders are frustrated as they try to persuade, manipulate, nudge, and push people in the organization. The people are angry, compliant, or disengaged. The organization feels cold—mechanical, political, Machiavellian, frustrating, and draining. That is what the absence of connectedness means.

When connectedness values are missing, we are not a community. We may be surrounded by people, but we feel like an island. We go home at the end of the day feeling as though no one cares about us, what is best for the customer and other stakeholders, and how we might improve. A great deal of research on the negative effects of social isolation suggests that it not only makes us hate our jobs but will actually shorten our life by roughly seven years and make us miserable and depressed. Lack of connection can actually kill us.[5]

Whether it is during a walk in the woods, at the breakfast table, or when sharing an experience while traveling, we have all experienced connectedness with family and friends and in romantic relationships. We know that grand gestures make a difference, but it's really the everyday actions, conversations, and ability to be ourselves with others that binds us to those we love.

At a very primal level, we humans are social animals who hunger for connection. Connecting is a powerful driver of innovation and success, and it has been that way for centuries. As Michael Chazan, an archaeologist who studies the evolution of humans, noted after a recent discovery of ash,

> The analysis pushes the timing for the human use of fire back by 300,000 years....
>
> [The control of fire] would have been a major turning point in human evolution....The impact of cooking food is well documented, but the impact of control over fire would have touched all elements of human society. [Furthermore,] socializing around a campfire might actually be an essential aspect of what makes us human.[6]

In our highly digitized society, our connections can be shallow and numerous rather than deep and meaningful. Our multitasking lifestyles combined with our use of technology can feed a one-way, staccato communication style. A real connection needs focus, attentiveness, time, and interest. It can be achieved through technology, but doing so requires a more holistic approach that often works best when grounded in a strong relational foundation that is achieved with two-way interaction and dialogue, whether through technology or face-to-face. Across all societies and all time, whether direct or virtual, no matter what the cultural context, we crave connectedness at some level. It is part of what makes us human.

Anthropologist Michael Tomasello has suggested that it is our ability to connect with others cooperatively that has been one of the main forces of human evolution and dominance.[7] Evolution has selected those who are "good cooperators," according to him. Evidence of how early humans hunted and shared equally the spoils of the hunt marks a real difference from how other great apes survived. Even the emergence of language points to the most powerful mechanism that we have for cooperation. When a child learns a word, she learns what the word does, the actions and reactions that are possible by using the word. It is easy to forget that using words is one of the main ways we work together and get things done. When we are at work, it is conversations, relationships, and trust that determine what does or does not get accomplished.

As leaders in organizations, we need to create nurturing and supportive environments that both respect and acknowledge the differences in what each of us needs to be successful. People experience the tension between collectivism and individual autonomy differently. Some people like constant conversations with one another, inspiring each other, solving problems together, and sharing the highs and the lows of life. Others are more introverted, excelling in quieter, lower-stimulation, and more-solitary conditions. A fundamental aspect of our role as leaders is to enable those we work with to connect as needed to make our organizations thrive.

The Benefits of Connectedness

Connectedness is important because it is part of the essence of what makes us human. Particularly in the fast-paced business contexts in which most organizations operate today, we need connectedness because that is how we can make smart decisions quickly. Embedding connectedness in our values conversations enables us to tap intelligence throughout the organization and work with one another to solve challenges, and it empowers people to make decisions as they need to. Interestingly, connections naturally bubble up between people unless they are thwarted and especially when they are cultivated. Sometimes connections within the organization are sparked by customers or other outside stakeholders, sometimes intentionally, sometimes unintentionally.

Connectedness is ongoing, self-organizing, and emergent. It leads to synergy where the organization, working collaboratively, is able to achieve profoundly more than do fragmented groups and individuals. Connectedness increases our ability to avoid duplication and reinventing the wheel. Organizations are innately collective and distributed, and our role as leaders in creating connectedness is to help these natural dynamics flourish. As Howard Schultz says about Starbucks, "Starbucks coffee is exceptional, yes, but *emotional connection* is our true value proposition."[8]

VTC Principles and Practices: Bridging the Values Gap by Bringing Connectedness Values to Life

How can we cultivate this kind of fulfilling and beneficial collaborative togetherness in our organizations? We suggest that it happens one conversation and one interaction at a time. Connectedness looks different in every organization, but we have found that some good practices often underpin connectedness in continuously successful ones.

Better Together

The starting point for understanding connectedness is often a strong sense of "we," a collective identity that forms a bond among people. Sometimes this bond is based on history, discussed in chapter 6, or a shared purpose, which we examine in chapter 8. Building and strengthening a collective identity requires caring for and looking after one another, having each other's back, working together to solve common challenges, goodwill, shared pride, and mutual support.

Every employee is invested in the common good and a shared future. We recognize that we are good individually but know that we are better together.

Creating a stronger sense of "we" may start with something pretty simple; sometimes we need to take baby steps. When David Elsner, as general manager of The Global Group of Companies, stepped into a new role, he noticed that there was a lack of synergy between management and plant employees. Somehow those clashes and tensions needed to be addressed. The Global Group is the fifth-largest multinational manufacturer, marketer, and distributor of office furniture and related products. The company is located in Toronto, and many employees play in hockey leagues in the winter—it's Canada. Elsner, a hockey player, decided that he would begin transforming how managers and plant employees interacted by converting the managers' lunchroom into a hockey bag storage room. Now managers would eat with plant employees in a communal lunchroom.

During the first week, there was resistance and division within the two groups. Elsner realized that for the change to work, unlearning of old habits and the freedom to challenge conformist perceptions would have to occur: "Managers who employ a robust presence and domineering managerial style prevent employees from taking additional responsibility. By stepping aside and nurturing conversations, they can create space for employees to become engaged and naturally fill operational gaps by challenging the fundamental assumptions."[9]

Sure enough, the front lines slowly began to share their views, and managers started asking questions and listening in a new way. Core assumptions were challenged, and the culture began to shift, as action-oriented solutions led to positive impacts and major breakthroughs. As Elsner notes, "This shared space created a method that provided an unassuming way of asking inquisitive questions that led to a systematic understanding of current issues and provided an approach to problem solving at both an operational and a strategic level. The shared lunchroom essentially changed the direction and the intensity of the vicious loop that impeded our growth." The establishment of the hockey bag storage room created space for empowerment to emerge by eradicating blockades. And with the success of the communal lunchroom, a more participative democratic employee-centered style of leadership emerged.

David Novak is CEO of Yum! Brands, which includes KFC, Taco Bell, Pizza Hut, Long John Silver's, and A&W All-American Food. In talking about KFC's turnaround, Novak says, "You must create owner-ship to keep employees invested in and excited about the success of the company." When things are not going so well, you ask for help and input. Bringing this value to life, when KFC faced a downward spi-ral Novak asked angry franchisees to pretend they were president of company, to meet and discuss what changes KFC needed, and to come back and tell him what the company's priorities should be. They gave him three priorities: improve quality, launch new products, and train people better. Novak listened, and KFC was transformed into a con-nected team with a common purpose and goals. Says Novak, "What ultimately turned KFC around? The finance people will tell you it was the new products we developed....But I always say it was a triumph of human spirit because we only developed those things once we started working together." There's a sign in the Yum! Brands lobby that reads, "Today's stock price is x, tomorrow's is up to you."[10]

Connectedness values help leaders build organizations that respect and value what everyone brings to the table. Leaders in con-nected organizations actively solicit input and engagement up, down, and across the company as well as beyond—to customers, other exter-nal stakeholders, and the communities in which we live.

Lululemon Athletica, the popular Canadian yoga-inspired cloth-ing retailer, realizes the power of "better together" and embeds com-munity connectedness into its process for opening new stores, which begins long before the doors open. Company managers invite local yoga instructors and fitness advocates, whom they call "ambassadors," to get to know Lululemon. They give them free apparel, ask for input on their products, and invite them to teach free classes at the new store. They post to their website YouTube videos of local ambassadors and often display large pictures of them in the stores. They do nearly zero mass advertising and instead invest time and money in local word-of-mouth networks, believing that personal relationships are more likely to fuel interest. Lululemon knows that when yogis have a personal connection with a community-based yoga instructor who is wearing Lululemon apparel, they are more likely to believe in the product.[11]

When Lululemon opened a new store in Chicago near Wrigley Field, it incorporated the local love of baseball in its messaging, with the words *yoga, run, love, baseball* on the store awning. It also held a massive yoga event at Wrigley Field itself, filling the entire stadium with folks doing the downward-facing dog. Former CEO Christine Day shared her leadership philosophy: "I'm not the big brain making every decision in the company. By actually giving that responsibility, letting the brand values live meaningfully at a local level, we keep our brand entrepreneurial. I'm always learning things from what they are doing, that we then take and amplify up."[12]

Lesia Dallimore, Lululemon's brand experience manager, says that the brand's social media engagement is important: "When you walk into a Lululemon store, we don't just want to hand you some gear, we want to chat with you, find out your goals. If you want to know the best place to get a coffee down the street, we want to tell you because we're experts in our community. And those are the same conversations we're having on Facebook."[13] For Lululemon, building connectedness within its community, whether in stores, on baseball fields, or online, fosters bonding with the brand and helps sell more yoga pants, too.

Another great example of how companies engage all stakeholders is through local and global give-back initiatives. Telus, a large telecommunications company with headquarters in British Columbia serving North and Central America, Asia Pacific, and Europe, embeds community grassroots engagement in a number of ways. This includes its annual international Day of Giving, which brings together thousands of local employees to help their communities, as well as the thousands of Christmas gifts they sent to families after the Philippines typhoon. It also involves treating orphans in Romania to a special day away from the institution, building homes for families in need in San Salvador, and planting nearly 10,000 trees and plants in a day in Canada. Many other companies engage in similar activities because, like Telus, they understand that being connected with local communities and helping solve global issues fuels passion and energy and enables us all to be better together.

Another powerful dimension of connectedness and creating a strong "we" is the sense that those in the organization have our backs and can be counted on in times of crisis. How Ratan Tata, chairman of the Tata Group of Industries, responded to the 2008 terrorist attack on one of its hotels, the Taj Mahal Palace Hotel in Mumbai, is a symbolic story of "we've got your back" in action. In the initial days after the attacks, employee outreach centers were created, offering help, food, sanitation, first aid, and counseling. Every employee was assigned a mentor to facilitate any assistance needed. Within 20 days, Tata created the Taj Public Service Welfare Trust to help employees; he also committed to providing for any education desired by the 46 children of the victims. In addition to a generous settlement for every deceased employee, he promised full salary and medical coverage for the family and dependents for the rest of their lives, as well as complete responsibility for the education of children and dependents anywhere in the world. All loans and advances were waived, irrespective of the amount, and a counselor for life was provided for each person.[14]

Although many companies face crises on a smaller scale, the key questions in terms of connectedness are the kinds of conversations these crises trigger and whether the company engages in actions that demonstrate its respect and accountability for its stakeholders: Do we cultivate ownership or pass the buck? Do we communicate openly and transparently and gather input and feedback from our stakeholders? Do we actively engage with our local communities? Do we take actions that prevent mistakes and crises from recurring?

In moments of crisis, our values become transparent to others. As crises unfold, some organizations and leaders, such as Ratan Tata, reach out and tap our hearts and spirits. For others, however, crises expose secrecy, deceit, and a lack of transparency, whether it is the cover-up of hundreds of lawsuit settlements by General Motors for exploding gas tanks or faulty ignitions[15] or former Mayor of Toronto Rob Ford's firing members of his executive committee who spoke up with concerns about his leadership when he was clearly derailing.

A strong collective identity also cultivates a sense of pride where everyone can be a hero. In many organizations connectedness is extended to only some stakeholders. Whether it is the folks in the mailroom, the custodial staff, the porters, or the secretaries, many organizations have "invisibles."

Zappos embraces all employees' contributions with its Hero Award employee recognition program. The online shoe retailer also has an initiative in which every employee is given $50 per month to give to a helpful or high-performing colleague as a bonus. The company selects its monthly hero by combing the list of people who received a co-worker bonus. The Hero Award winner is selected from the pool of employees who have already been recognized by their co-workers. The monthly hero is announced with a mini-parade, noisemakers, and the song "I Need a Hero" playing. The chosen hero receives a covered parking spot for a month, a $150 Zappos gift card, and a cape.[16] For some this kind of behavior may seem corny or over the top, but the underlying theme that everyone is a hero and a shared, decentralized method for choosing the heroes fosters connectedness and enables "better together" at Zappos.

Thus, whether it is de-escalating a sit-in, establishing a shared lunchroom, building community support, taking care of employees in times of crisis, celebrating an employee hero of the month, or hosting retreats, town halls, or weekly meetings, VTC on connectedness is how we create solidarity and a collective "we" that trumps ego.

Relational Work Is Real Work

Working together requires connectedness. In many organizations there is a bifurcation between rational work and social time. Yet, what if we saw relational work as the *real* work of organizations? Many companies have invested a great deal of time and money in cultivating a relationship mind-set for their customers, but internally it might be a different story. Building strong, resilient relationships and this relational work is another aspect of what connectedness values are all about.

Have you ever been in a meeting where there is tons of tension and nobody respects or even likes one another? Not much happens. Contrast that with a meeting where everybody can be themselves, share ideas, problem-solve, and know that conflicting perspectives will not lead to back stabbing and undermining. Without the ability to work together, not much gets done. Whether it is business at the bar, deals on the golf course, rock wall climbing, or whitewater rafting, relational activities refuel us, enable us to work more productively, and often get more "real work" done than time at our desks.

We need to nurture the ability to have those real relationships all the time and recognize how important they are to our feeling good about what we do. We need to be able to be ourselves with those around us. There should not be thought bubbles over our heads like cartoon characters, capturing what we really feel while contrary words are coming out of our mouths. That is not good for us personally or for the organizations in which we spend our time.

We've been testing the idea that relational work is real work in our MBA classes on strategic change with a course component called *building community*. In each class there is a randomly assigned team of students responsible for leading the community building for that session. As the class begins, they play a song that relates to leading change and strategic evolution. Songs include "Imagine" by John Lennon, "Lean on Me" by Bill Withers, Bob Marley's "One Love," and "Do You Hear the People Sing?" from *Les Miserables*. The team for that week also shares a quote from someone they admire, such as Nelson Mandela, Thomas Edison, Albert Einstein, Margaret Mead, Jay-Z, Abraham Lincoln, or their mom. They then share with the class why they chose the song and the quotation, what about the words and music resonates with them, and how it relates to the course from their perspective.

At the break they lead a community-building activity; it could be building marshmallow towers with toothpicks, creating a bobsled race using PVC pipe and a marble, finding your herd (giving everyone animal cards and asking them to find others who are the same animal without making a sound), or teaching different subgroups different parts of a Boxercise dance. Some might suggest that this wastes valuable class time, but, interestingly, in a commuter MBA program in a second-year elective where few people know each other, spending just 15 minutes out of a weekly three-hour class doing these activities fosters a classroom community that thrives; this is indicated by team project results, student testimonials, and end-of-term performance metrics for both the course and the students.

Comments from student feedback include how safe the environment is, how the class feels like a family, the power of the un-MBA way of learning, the kindness and genuine concern, the strong sense of community even though students didn't know one another when the course started, and how this simple activity helps everyone talk with one another, and work better together in and outside the classroom.[17]

Many business schools have their students engage in community activities, whether building and repairing houses for low-income people, serving on social-sector boards, sponsoring auctions to raise money for women's shelters, or mentoring students in local public schools. Often seen as fluff or wasted time, such activities can actually be powerful bond builders that improve individual, team, and organizational outcomes.

Companies get into the act as well, whether it's blowing giant bubbles at a retreat; corporate campuses with gyms, fitness classes, swimming pools, bikes, and volleyball courts like at Facebook and Google's Googleplex; or GoDaddy's whitewater rafting trips. Such companies understand that play enhances connectedness and enables us to work better together. Carey Mullett, an employee at Patagonia, says about the team of 20-plus people who go on climbing excursions to test out Patagonia equipment and bond, "It's hard for people who are used to a fixed itinerary to understand, but it's this kind of deconstruction that leads to the most creative work."[18]

We all understand that integrating play into our day makes us more creative and productive. A half hour of enrichment yields better outcomes the rest of the day. That is why we encourage kids at school to have recess, gym, art, music, and other enjoyable activities. Indeed, as Adele Diamond, a leading cognitive neuroscientist, says, "If we want the best academic outcomes, the most efficient and cost-effective route to achieve that is, counterintuitively, *not* to narrowly focus on academics, but to also address children's social, emotional, and physical development."[19]

Meaningful outreach to one another seems to matter to us all, whether it is writing a thank-you note or visiting frontline employees to congratulate them for a job well done. Many of the most successful CEOs realize that teleprompters and online videocasts are pretty cold. They prefer face time and heartfelt messages and notes.

Robert Kapito, founder and president of BlackRock, a trillion-dollar global asset management firm, says, "I bring our emerging leaders to my house. I cook for them. They get to know me as a person, not just a role. Trust is built by people being transparent and authentic with one another. Authenticity has high currency at BlackRock."[20]

Connectedness thrives when people do what they are good at and there is transparency, trust, and shared ownership, accountability, and leadership. Shared leadership does not mean, however, that everybody leads everything and everyone has to be consulted on every decision. It means we each should lead things we are good at. On some projects or initiatives, we will be leaders; on others we will be followers. And sometimes we'll do a bit of both. Whether we are leading or following, we will be more effective and authentic when we feel embedded in a community of mutual respect and activity and conversations are geared toward things that matter to us.

Beyond hearing multiple voices, connectedness also works better if we feel we are in a nurturing context for speaking up and offering our perspective. As leaders we need to work at cultivating conversations and developing communication channels to ensure that a multiplicity of voices can be heard, as in the Colgate University sit-in example at the beginning of this chapter.

Education, awareness, and access to information are crucial for enabling people throughout an organization to contribute. For us to be connected, we need to feel we are able to engage in respectful dialogue with transparency, creating space for each person's capabilities and personality and cultivating our own skills and growth so that we and the organization can thrive. Dissent is not only tolerated but seen as the fuel of innovation and improvement. That might mean changing how we run meetings to open up the agenda, validating conflicting viewpoints, rotating a devil's advocate role, and building in space for all voices to be heard. Simple techniques such as generating ideas individually with sticky notes and posting them for discussion might create space for suppressed voices and ideas to come to the fore.

After all of these inspiring ideas about connectedness, we might be thinking, *But I have to do rounds and rounds of layoffs in the coming months. What should I do about connectedness?* First of all, many organizations overlook the direct costs of layoffs, which include out-placement and severance, paying out accrued vacation and sick days, higher unemployment-insurance taxes, and the cost of rehiring when business improves. Now take into account the indirect costs: low morale and productivity, anxiety, potential lawsuits and sabotage, diminished trust, loss of organizational knowledge and memory, the best employees exiting and the health impact on those who remain, survivor's guilt, and wondering *Will I be next?* These are real budget suckers. Indeed, research shows negative stock returns for layoffs over the long run and that downsizing in general reduces profitability, particularly in research-and-development-intensive industries.[21] Firing is not the panacea it might appear to be.

We might consider alternatives to layoffs, such as four-day work-weeks, increased nonpaid vacation days, nonproduction days, and voluntary packages. We could also try working together to cut costs and cultivate additional connectedness, which perhaps might result in more than we ever imagined and enable us to avoid layoffs altogether. For example, Teranet, an international leader and pioneer in electronic land registration systems and commerce, uncovered thousands of dollars' worth of savings because of a dispute over who was to pay for an invoice for Yellow Pages advertising. Once the procurement manager took a longer look, she realized that they had been paying for Yellow Pages advertising for 10 years. Just by canceling the advertising, they saved $44,000 annually. This triggered the realization that there were likely many similar opportunities for cost savings throughout the company.

Teranet executives were smart enough to realize that discovering other savings like this would have to be a decentralized, bottom-up effort or it would undermine the trust and engagement they had built throughout the company. Their solution was twofold.

First, they made the initiative highly visible, with heavy incentives to perform. It was a corporate balanced scorecard (BSC) measure with a target of 150 implemented improvements with no restrictions on the type or size of initiative; they wanted to encourage employees to focus on the little details and ensure that everyone could contribute. Many managers received bonuses partially based on this BSC measure. Additionally, this was one of the four measures determining the year-end profit-sharing bonus that all employees are eligible to receive, which usually adds up to about two weeks' pay. They also conducted periodic draws during town hall meetings, where they threw all the submitted initiatives into a hat and did a random drawing to win a coffee gift card or similar small item.

Second, they gave each department a rough quota and encouraged side bets and contests with other teams. Having friendly rivalries and wagers helped the teams to get into the action. Teranet ended up with more than 300 implemented improvements during the first year, doubling the target of 150. The company's headcount was approximately 350 at the time, so it had nearly one improvement per employee on average.

The following year it kept a similar measure but changed the focus slightly to concentrate on improvements meeting a certain threshold: a cost savings of more than $10,000 or cycle time improvement of greater than 25 percent. This shift in focus was made for two reasons: to get staff thinking bigger and to encourage teamwork across all departments. Most initiatives meeting the threshold would require the cooperation of multiple teams, so this worked well with the other corporate priority, which was to support enhanced teamwork. The company kept the natural rivalries and side bets, however, to maintain friendly competition. It again exceeded the target, with many more implemented improvements than expected.

You might be wondering why a discussion about the detrimental impact of layoffs and alternatives is in a book about narrowing the values gap. Usually, but not always, financial downturns in organizations are one of those pivotal moments where everyone is watching to see whether the company will live its values or whether the gap between the talk and the walk will widen. So, as good leaders a first question to ask is whether the effects on connectedness and community and the downside costs of any layoffs being considered have been factored in. Another question is whether there are creative alternatives, such as reducing workweeks, making pay cuts, or, as Teranet did, engaging employees on cost cutting to streamline processes and save money.

If we still need to lay off employees, there are better and worse ways to do it. Better ways include transparency on who and why and not leaving people—both those being laid off and those being retained—in limbo, wondering whether they will survive the cut. Better might also mean letting people manage their own exits, taking the time and the emotional energy to have face-to-face transition meetings, cutting at all levels and not just the front line, being as generous as possible with severance pay, and hiring high-quality outplacement services.

Fundamentally, every interaction at work is either supporting or thwarting our relationships. Those companies that recognize and embrace the notion that relational work is real work, and part of the engine of connectedness, understand that time invested in cultivating relationships and bonding pays off with benefits far beyond what we might imagine. That includes how we handle situations in which cost cutting needs to happen. The actions we take in these everyday decisions and as well as in the context of more-momentous crises tell the organization what we really stand for and either bridge or widen the values gap.

Being One's Whole Self

We all know that when things are not going well at home, it can spill over into other spheres of our lives. Similarly, when things are not going well at work, our family relationships might be affected. Sometimes we can compartmentalize, compensate in one sphere for problems in another, or successfully bifurcate our personal and work lives, but usually that does not work well nor can it last very long. Part of what keeps us whole is our ability to bring our entire selves home and bring our full selves to work. There is a lot of discussion about valuing diversity, but this is more nuanced. Being one's whole self means trusting that we can be who we are and that that will be appreciated. It involves accepting others as whole people where there is psychological safety for all. We feel as though we can reveal our whole selves, reach out to others as needed, and trust that sharing our feelings will not be used against us.

At a large global consumer company we have worked with, connectedness is sometimes nurtured through such practices as "head, heart, and hands" check-ins, where people go around the table and share what is going on in their lives, from family, to work outside the meeting, to their health or other top-of-mind issues, as well as their feelings about the work that has brought them together. This type of exercise enables people to bring and be their whole selves in the workplace, with recognition of the myriad other responsibilities we all have. It takes up meeting time, but this company and others that engage in similar connectedness practices agree that it saves time in the end by reducing cross-functional conflict, streamlining work processes, and building camaraderie and friendships.

Language in our conversations facilitates connectedness as well. For example, being able to use the word *squeeze*—as in, "I'm having a bit of a squeeze on this," which in essence means *This doesn't sit quite right with me and here's why* without criticizing the person—facilitates more open and honest discussions that are the fuel for connectedness.

In and out is another phrase that is part of connectedness language in this organization. "I'm in" tells everyone that I'm focused on the work at hand. "I'm out" tells everyone that for this hour or this morning or this week I am distracted because of other work or outside life priorities. For example, at a retreat I helped facilitate, one top leader was out because of a work-related crisis she was handling on the other side of the world. Another was out because his son was fighting cancer.

Cycles of life happen while we are working for organizations. The question for us as leaders is whether we will try to embrace these life events or suppress them and pretend they aren't happening. Having babies and taking care of aging parents are other life events that often occur while we are immersed in our careers. Companies that embrace such life changes with support and flexibility enable that whole-self feeling.

PricewaterhouseCoopers, for example, has a mentoring program that matches expectant or adoptive mothers with other moms at the company who can offer parenting wisdom and guidance through conversations about the firm's maternity policies. The Mentor Moms program starts four months before maternity leave and lasts until a baby's first birthday. For those who want more time off, the company offers all employees the option to take five years away from the job for dependent care reasons (usually a child or parent), with a good-faith guarantee that they will be able to return. For new and expectant parents at Facebook, "it doesn't get much better than this: Four months paid parental leave, reimbursement for daycare and adoption fees and $4,000 'baby cash' for your new arrival."[22]

Taking care of parents is another issue that many baby boomers are struggling with as they try to integrate the demands of high-powered careers with being there for their aging parents. Progressive companies understand the pressures of this stage of life and provide support. Conversations about these types of life events in such companies become commitment reaffirming rather than alienating.

Contrast this with the boss who says, "Oh, my god, no!" when he learns that an executive is pregnant with her second child. Or consider an organization in which a colleague dies of heart attack; her work is being discussed in a meeting, which stirs sad feelings among those on the team, and the person running the meeting discounts the emotions and proceeds with the agenda.

Sometimes people cannot make their whole lives work with being in the organization. They feel unable to share their challenges with anyone, so they exit. Many companies are working hard to provide flexible hours and help those inside their organizations do what they need to do. If we are losing good employees, we should make serious efforts to understand why. Of course, it might be salary or advancement issues, but a key and often-overlooked driver of turnover is whether employees feel that they have the flexibility and support they need to attend to their family, friends, passions, and other outside commitments—in short, whether they can be *whole* at work. The more whole they feel, the more connected they are, and that often translates into difficult-to-cultivate dedication and commitment.

Conclusion

As we have seen with the stories and examples in this chapter, connectedness values focus on conversations about how we lead, make decisions, organize and plan our work, generate ideas, support one another on a daily basis and when facing crises, and evolve individually and collectively. These values ask how we bring our whole selves and our values to life within our community. Organizations that do this well lean toward connection that is mutual, collective, and ongoing. It involves working together to co-create meaningful services and products that better the world in a community of respect, with shared ownership and distributed responsibility.

Questions to be asked as part of this dialogue might include who our stakeholders are and how will we connect, coordinate, and build relationships with each of them. We might also ask what we mean by "relationships" and how we cultivate shared leadership to ensure that multiple perspectives are heard. As individuals and as a community, how will we support new ideas, innovation, and change? And how will we nurture our whole selves—our heads and our hearts and our hands—through our work. In short, how will we be better together?

CONVERSATION STARTERS FOR CONNECTEDNESS VALUES

Bridging the values gap through how we have conversations, interact, lead, follow, and work together to achieve our collective purpose and aspirations

- Who are our stakeholders, and how will we connect, coordinate, and build relationships with each of them?
- How will we cultivate collective leadership?
- Who are the "invisibles" in our organization? How can we change that?
- How can we encourage dialogue that fosters community within our organization?
- How do we ensure that multiple perspectives are nurtured?
- How will we learn, innovate, and change?
- How will we cultivate innovation and new ideas?
- How will we ensure that we bring our whole selves to the organization?
- How will we communicate?
- How should power be distributed?
- How do we make decisions?
- Are we recognized and rewarded for our relational work and community building?
- Do we have tools and processes that enable people to collaborate and connect across locations and functions?
- Do we have flexibility in how we structure our work lives to support our whole life?
- What conversations are we avoiding or feel we cannot begin? What are the costs of *not* talking about those things?
- Can we usually say what we are thinking?

CHAPTER 8

Aspirational Values: Our Hopes and Dreams

American historian, poet, and novelist Carl Sandburg wrote, "Nothing happens unless first a dream."[1] How do we articulate a dream for an organization? One powerful way is through aspirations that capture who we are and what we stand for and why. Usually, to figure out what that dream might be we need to collectively ask, *Why do we exist?* In this chapter we explore the aspirational aspects of values through conversation that help us bring our organizational dreams to life.

The Role of Aspirations in Values through Conversation

Aspirations are discussed in many organizations but often take the form of a vision statement that focuses primarily on market and competitive positioning. These types of vision statements emphasize how the company is the first-choice brand or the most profitable in the industry or how the company guarantees excellent service to its customers. The vision is more of a marketing tool than inspirational guide. These types of vision statements, while sometimes helpful to the consumer, feel shallow and hollow to stakeholders such as employees. Although some companies have expanded the scope of their vision beyond competitive positioning and customers to include statements

---

AT A GLANCE: ASPIRATIONAL VALUES

Bridging the values gap by collectively building our hopes, dreams, purpose, and how we see ourselves as contributing to our stakeholders and the greater good over time

Benefits

- Clear priorities
- Values compass
- Passion for the cause
- Inspiration and meaning
- Focus and dedication
- Bettering the world

Principles

- Do good, do better
- Bridging personal growth and organizational growth
- Reinspiring aspiration and purpose

Practices

- Put value creation first
- Create greater-good benefits in products, services, and processes
- Develop an inspiring mantra
- Foster personal growth
- Reach out to stakeholders to see how and whether the vision is being lived
- Reinspire aspirations regularly

---

about how they aspire to treat employees and other stakeholders, many of those statements still feel empty and uninspired. This connection between being inspired and developing aspiration is strong and not well understood.

When employees and leaders are inspired, they are able to set their aspirations at a high level. Some organizations know how to combine aspiration and inspiration in a winning cycle. Inspired people keep raising the bar for themselves and the organization. This is what happens at companies such as Whole Foods Market, Starbucks, Steam Whistle Brewing, O.Noir, Berrett-Koehler, and Princess Margaret Cancer Centre. Their aspirations are meaningful guideposts for action and decision making in the company.

Aspirations represent our collective passion and purpose, painting a picture of the future we want. They convey how we as a company make a difference to all of our stakeholders and why our efforts will make the world a better place. VTC on aspirations involves an ongoing exploration in concert with changing context, needs, and demands that help us articulate how we make a difference and why we exist. Meaningful aspirations help us take actions that not only shape our future but also engage and inspire others to join us, and they provide an anchor in a world of constant change.

The Benefits of Aspiration

We need aspirations so we know what we are working toward and have a sense of purpose. Aspirations give us a personal and organizational compass that guides our decisions, choices, actions, and behaviors and keeps us moving toward our common goals. Energy and passion are the fuel that fires up our organizations. Usually, that passion stems from more than the bottom line. For us to feel intense dedication, our work in organizations needs to matter and make a difference. We need the organizations we work for to collectively contribute something meaningful, inspiring, and important to the world. That is what ignites our passion and attracts the best talent. That sense of meaningful purpose makes everything we do more joyful.

Even with two companies that may have equally talented people and innovative products or services, the key differentiator in business that determines success is not so much our resources or capabilities but our mind-set. Aspirations often provide that uplifting frame on what we are doing that enables us to reach our goals and even beyond.

Determination, dedication, focus, and believing that we can bring our aspirations to life are powerful secret weapons that are unbeatable.

When aspirational values are missing, the organization has no rudder. Everyone is doing his or her own thing. There is no center to the organization, no heart and soul. In the worst-case scenario, it results in disasters like Enron, notorious for its unethical accounting practices and institutional fraud. "Instead of seeing money as a reward for doing something meaningful, it became an end in itself."[2]

While Enron was values-empty in the extreme, the reality for the majority of employees is that they have no sense of how what they do connects to their companies' priorities. A Towers Watson 2012 Global Workforce Study of 32,000 employees in medium and large companies from 29 countries around the world found that just over one-third—35 percent—of employees were highly engaged at work, whether in growth or recessionary economies. The study also found that feeling connected to one's company's priorities strongly influences absenteeism, "presenteeism" (low productivity at work), turnover, and the bottom line. Indeed, this study reveals that close to 75 percent of disengaged employees would not hesitate to leave for a comparable opportunity elsewhere.[3] How we engage those in our organizations is a complex question, but strong, achievable, understandable, and meaningful aspirations are certainly part of the puzzle, along with a bond to our history and connectedness as well as time for introspection, as discussed in earlier chapters.

At a personal level, a lot of research says that we are our happiest when we set meaningful aspirational goals and achieve them.[4] To attain our goals, we often need to translate them into concrete actions. Saying that we are going to "give back more" this year may be aspirational, but it may not happen unless we think about our purpose in life, who our personal stakeholders are, and where and how we can make an impact. It might be building a business that transforms some aspect of society for the better, joining a social-sector board, or doing a small act of kindness each day. Regardless of the specifics, having that aspiration and working toward it will make us happier and more fulfilled and contribute beyond that.

The same is true for organizations. Aspiration helps in giving us direction, so we know the path we are headed on and why. We will likely need to translate that overarching vision into specific attainable objectives with timelines through conversations with different stakeholder groups. What is key is that the connection between what we do and how we achieve our higher-level vision in unison should be apparent. Without that direction on where we are headed and why, we will likely work aimlessly, unable to navigate or prioritize, and not really progress.

The bottom line is that purposelessness is soul sapping. We all have a deep need for finding something meaningful and for being valued as well as paying life forward. Without that we are a bit lost. While the specific words chosen for a vision or statement of aspirations are clearly important, what is more important is the process of how the values are developed, translated into action, and evolve. For aspirations to be collectively inspiring, they cannot be handed down by executives or some task force. They need to be pondered, debated, and jointly contributed to, so our aspirations have shared authorship and ownership in how they are enacted.

VTC Principles and Practices: Bridging the Values Gap by Bringing Aspirational Values to Life

To be meaningful, aspirations should be driven by a powerful *why* and a collective *What do we stand for?* that resonates with us and inspires us to achieve our highest potential. Aspirations are not telling us what to do, but rather guiding and pulling us forward. This *why* often is the most compelling when it combines a powerful story with strong business reasoning and analytics. A catchy three- or four-word mantra to center us around the aspiration often helps, as well, whether it's Nike's *Just do it,* FedEx's *Peace of mind,* Apple's *Think different,* or Whole Foods Market's *Whole foods, whole people, whole planet.*

This combination of head and heart helps paint an inspiring picture of the future. Knowing that the work we are doing betters the world also galvanizes us. Making a difference matters.

Alignment of personal goals and organizational goals is critical, too. Alignment creates synergy between personal growth and organizational growth. We are excited and motivated because we are achieving new individual heights, and our work helps our organization and the stakeholders we are connected to reach their potential and contribute something valuable.

Sometimes organizations lose their purpose and derail. Having clear aspirations is extremely beneficial then, as well. Clear and strong aspirations help us understand when we go off the tracks. We then will likely need to reinspire our aspirations to recenter and regain momentum. Let's take a look at some of the good practices that we have observed as we think about the aspirational part of bridging the values gap through conversation.

Do Good, Do Better

There has been a lot of chatter in recent years about shareholder value versus stakeholder value. That dichotomy misses the point that if we focus on a "win, win, win, win, win" approach, as John Mackey, co-founder and co-CEO of Whole Foods Market calls it, we will also find ourselves with high shareholder returns. Or as we recently noted, "We need red blood cells to live, the same way a business needs profits to live, but the purpose of life is more than to make red blood cells, the same way the purpose of business is more than simply to generate profits."[5] Yes, making money is vital, but focusing on "doing good" and bettering people's lives gives us the meaning and purpose that keeps us inspired and energized.

Research confirms that companies that do good and make a difference in the world do better. In a study of companies that focus on a sense of purpose and on all of their stakeholders, Raj Sisodia, David Wolfe, and Jag Sheth found that these companies radically outperform the major stock indexes.[6] Employees are even willing to take a pay cut if their companies do good.[7]

It used to be that doing good was a sideshow for most organizations, but these days many companies understand that when doing good is woven into the fabric of every action and decision, the company and everyone connected to it benefits. If we have a powerful purpose, that fires us up and the profits follow. Whether it's Whole Foods Market bringing healthy eating to North America or Merck curing river blindness in remote communities in Africa, Latin America, and the Middle East, these companies know that bettering the world betters their organizations. They go beyond passive responsibility and causing no harm to proactive responsibility and making the world a better place. These companies see how business might be able to revolutionize the world for the better while protecting the planet. They focus on making meaningful contributions to themselves, their stakeholders, and their communities—all with an eye on future generations. That is where aspiration and inspiration meld together to foster passion and creativity.

Whole Foods Market is a fabulous example of a company guided by not just profits but a higher purpose, stakeholder orientation, and a conscious leadership and culture. John Mackey opened his first store in meat-loving Texas in 1980. The mantra *Whole foods, whole people, whole planet* captures the company's higher purpose and vision of bringing healthy foods and eating habits to society. Mackey said in a profile in the *New Yorker,* "Business serves society. It produces goods and services that make people's lives better....Whole Foods puts food on people's tables and we improve people's health. We provide jobs. We provide capital through profits that spur improvements in the world.

And we're good citizens in the communities; we take our citizenship very seriously."[8]

It has worked well. Whole Foods is synonymous with organic, healthy food, and it has nearly 300 stores and billions in annual sales. "Our success in fulfilling our vision is measured by customer satisfaction, team member happiness and excellence, return on capital investment, improvement in the state of the environment, and local and larger community support."[9] It has low turnover in its executive ranks, and its "associates" have chosen not to unionize, rare in the grocery industry. But Whole Foods cannot sit on its laurels; the healthy-food movement it catalyzed has also encouraged more and more competitors. That is good for the people and the planet, and it keeps Whole Foods ever innovating.

So how does Whole Foods weave its aspirations into the company culture? What makes aspirational organizations great is not the words they use but how they live them. Mackey demonstrates his dedication to the cause with an annual salary of $1. The company connects with local growers and buys locally grown food that enables it to build ties in the community, lower transportation costs, reduce its carbon footprint, and boost local economies. Indeed, it has expanded the go-local commitment by creating a local producer loan program. Another way it supports local communities is through its 5 percent days, where 5 percent of store sales go to a local nonprofit or educational organization. Many Whole Foods stores also run Nickels for Nonprofits programs, where, if you bring your own reusable bag, Whole Foods gives you a nickel to keep or donate to a local nonprofit organization. Through these actions the company lives its values and connects its customers to their communities.

In addition, Whole Foods Market is embarking on an innovation in urban rooftop agriculture. In partnership with Gotham Greens Farms, it recently completed a 20,000-square-foot commercial-scale rooftop greenhouse for its Brooklyn store, where it grows pesticide-free greens that are sold in its area stores. This exciting partnership may help spur a revolution in the industry with urban rooftop farms that will produce healthy organic food to offset the concrete jungle. Here again, we see how actions Whole Foods takes reinforce its values to the benefit of its stakeholders and the planet.

Whole Foods is also active in *upcycling*—repurposing a waste object by valuing the material from which it is made and the form that the material is in. The company is converting used materials, such as the University of Virginia's basketball court floorboards and old bleachers, into picnic table tops in the Charlottesville store and saving money too. In California, the company installed energy management systems and data loggers to track how much energy its new refrigeration systems are saving. Whole Foods purchases renewable energy credits to offset 100 percent of the electricity used in its stores, and it ranks at the top of the 20 leading US purchasers of green power, according to the Environmental Protection Agency.[10]

Since Whole Foods Market's initial public offering, 93 percent of the stock options awarded have gone to nonexecutive team members. A salary cap limits the cash compensation, including wages plus bonuses, to 19 times the average of all full-time team members. Its financial books are open and list all compensation for everyone.

Recently, the company launched a program called Whole Cities to open stores in so-called food deserts. Stores have opened in inner-city Detroit and New Orleans's Ninth Ward, and there are plans to open stores in Newark and South Side Chicago. These are just some examples of the initiatives and ongoing actions that illustrate how Whole Foods really lives its vision and brings its values to life.

Another example of a company's building aspirational values and doing good is the development of a sustainable beer call Steam Whistle. Steam Whistle Brewing was a dream that began as Greg Taylor, Cam Heaps, and Greg Cromwell sat around a campfire after being fired from Sleeman Brewery as a result of an acquisition. Together they founded Steam Whistle Brewing. *3FG* (three fired guys) is stamped on every bottle to remind them of their roots and their history. Every beer is brewed with all-natural ingredients. They use bottles that can be recycled three times more than the industry standard. The factory is deep-water cooled from Lake Ontario rather than from air conditioning in summer. The brewery transports its products in biodiesel trucks and retrofitted electric vehicles, and it was the first brewery in Canada to use compostable beer cups.

The company encourages its employees to bike to work, so it provides showers, towels, and a safe-bike service. Six years after its founding, it won an award for being the best locally produced beer in Toronto. A year later it won for the best Pilsner beer. And the next year, it joined the top 10 best-selling premium beers in Ontario. Steam Whistle Brewing is a success story for its customers and employees because of the sustainable values embedded in every decision and discussion it has on how to run its business.

O.Noir, a restaurant in Toronto where you eat your dinner in absolute darkness and where the wait staff are visually disabled, is another example of do good, do better and how a series of conversations about how to live personal and business values can lead to a thriving venture. In the highly competitive and saturated food and beverage business, O.Noir is managing to survive longer than the average restaurant. As owner Moe Alameddine says, "When you eat food in the dark, your remaining senses are heightened...."[11] An added bonus is that every meal supports the greater good and social cause of providing employment for typically underemployed visually disabled people. There are similar restaurants in Montreal, Paris, London, and Rome.

Through these stories of Whole Foods, Steam Whistle Brewing, and O.Noir, we see how brilliant entrepreneurs began aspirational conversations that started their ventures. We also are offered insights into how they embed continuous conversations about their aspirations into their everyday practices and their evolution over time.

Bridging Personal Growth and Organizational Growth

For aspirations to truly be ignited, meeting aspirational goals should also be personally fulfilling for the people in the organization. AS CEO Jim Goodnight of SAS notes, "Ninety-five percent of my assets drive out the gate every evening. It's my job to maintain a work environment that keeps those people coming back every morning."[12] SAS fosters both personal and professional growth and offers employees subsidized Montessori child care, unlimited sick days, a free healthcare center, intramural sports teams, and no-cost work/life counseling to help effectively manage the stresses of everyday life. Earning recognition for a comprehensive and desirable work environment and benefits offering, SAS has consistently earned top placement in the Great Place to Work Institute's annual list of the world's best multinational workplaces. *Fast Company* recently called Google "an early emulator of SAS's practices."[13]

Another company that has woven personal growth with professional growth is Starbucks, which recently announced the benefit of two years' free tuition for all employees with no strings attached, which is pretty amazing given that 70 percent of Starbucks's employees are young or low-skilled workers who are in pursuit of postsecondary education. CEO Howard Schultz said of Starbucks's partnership with Arizona State University, "The only way you can build a great enduring company is by linking shareholder value with value for employees."[14]

We might wonder what inspires an organization to introduce a benefit plan promoting broad well-being and professional development with a direct cash cost and no direct cash benefit. Howard Schultz's aspiration stems in part from his childhood experience of having a father who was loyal to a series of blue-collar jobs without security or a safety net. Schultz has alluded to being deeply affected by his family's struggle when his father sustained a work-related injury and did not have health insurance or worker's compensation. Years later, when Schultz became CEO of Starbucks, catalyzed by conversations he had with employees, he extended the education benefit program even to temporary summer employees.

Commenting on this latest free tuition program, Schultz describes it as, "rebuilding the American Dream for employees, known as 'partners,' who are left behind in an economy that requires a degree… [in a country where] the cost of education can be prohibitive."[15]

Lululemon Athletica, the yoga-inspired apparel company highlighted in chapter 7, more explicitly leverages its fundamental values to bring together personal and professional growth for employees. Since its beginning in 1998, Lululemon has emphasized and embraced the importance of goal setting and achievement to reach personal aspirations. In its new employee orientation, staff members are invited to develop and post one-, five-, and 10-year personal, professional, and health targets. For employees with at least one year of seniority, a three-day off-site training program underscoring self-actualization coaches employees on how to achieve their personal goals while working at Lululemon. This is a lovely example of creating reflective time and space to converse about charting a path where both personal and organizational aspirations are achieved.[16]

Thus bridging personal and organizational growth enables employees to clearly see their *What's in it for me?* benefits. When personal and organizational growth are intertwined, there are other advantages, as well. Often companies that invest in the growth of their employees have among the lowest reported turnover rates in their industries.

Reinspiring Aspiration and Purpose

Sometimes we are starting from scratch as we move toward developing our first compelling aspirations and vision. Those early entrepreneurial days are often exciting, full of hope and optimism about a new product or service we are convinced the world needs. Other times we are revisiting our aspirations to reassess whether they still make sense or need to be rejiggered to meet changing times.

Now and then vision statements must evolve to stay abreast of external changes. We should anchor our aspirations in history and the roots of the organization, but we also need to grow, develop, and evolve without being restrained by aspirations that may need reframing or even revamping. Much more difficult is the challenge of reinspiring and reenergizing a failing organization that is filled with fear.

But Starbucks did it. We have touched on Starbucks with some examples of how the company has crowdsourced introspections from its customers and how it builds and leverages connections with its stakeholders. It is also a great example of a company that achieved an aspirational reboot. Starbucks's mission to "inspire and nurture the human spirit—one person, one cup and one neighborhood at a time" was about "bringing the magic and romance of an Italian espresso bar and coffee house with coffee at the center of conversation" to coffee drinkers in North America and to "create another 'home' filled with conversation for those who visited the coffee shop filled with a little luxury."[17] CEO Howard Schultz transformed a little-known local coffee shop into a leading retailer of specialty coffee in North America. Although Starbucks is again doing well, it was not in 2007 and 2008. Sales plummeted and stock prices dropped. Starbucks's global operating income in April 2008 was down 26 percent, a shock for a longtime success story and a first in Starbucks history.

As Schultz explained to Oprah, "We had lost our way. The pursuit of profit became our reason for being, and that is not the reason that Starbucks is in business...we're in the business of exceeding the expectations of our customers." Starbucks's decline was spurred by the combination of many factors, which Schultz called a "perfect storm of external pressures and self-induced imperfections."[18] The company had made poor real estate choices and overexpanded to reach 2,300 stores. It had weak internal accountability and outdated equipment. In a leaked e-mail to senior executives in 2007, Schultz slammed the "commoditization of the Starbucks experience" and the loss of the magic and romance: "We desperately need to look into the mirror and realize it's time to get back to the core...to evoke the heritage, the tradition, and the passion that we all have for the true Starbucks experience."[19]

Many leaders facing such a crisis and decline would be tempted to slash and burn. Schultz, however, searched for how to maintain the brand and sustain a culture of humanity as he closed stores, laid off employees, and then tried to reignite the company. What he did was unconventional—and brilliant. He planned a four-day retreat in New Orleans in the middle of a recession, when the city was still recovering from Hurricane Katrina. He invited 10,000 Starbucks partners. Why spend all that money to bring them all there? He said, "For all the promise of digital media to bring people together, I still believe that the most sincere, lasting powers of human connection come from looking directly into someone else's eyes, with no screen in between."[20]

When these Starbucks stakeholders arrived at the airport, a marching band greeted them with signs that said "Believe." *Believe* and *Onward* were their inspirational mantras for the week. Each stakeholder received a welcome bag and was invited to informational sessions, roundtables, and panels as well as four huge interactive galleries designed to reinspire the mission, values, operations, and new store management skills. There were community volunteer events to help hurricane-shattered New Orleans and four blocks of street fairs. T-shirts said "Onward" instead of "Starbucks." "If done right—and it had to be done right—a leadership conference would be a galvanizing event, raising our company's level of passion and performance where we needed it most: in front of our customers."[21]

The questions asked at this retreat are great VTC questions for a company trying to rediscover and re-create its aspirations:

- How could we create and improve the store experience which is our heritage and the foundation of the brand's identity?

- How might we expand on our value proposition which has always been about emotional and human connection?

- How should we strengthen our voice to better tell our story?

- How can the company extend its coffee authority beyond the stores?[22]

To help filter their responses to these questions, they asked essential aspirational questions about any idea suggested: "Will it make our people proud? Will this make the customer experience better? And will this enhance Starbucks in the minds and hearts of our customers?"[23] In the words of Schultz:

> I had to raise tens of thousands of spirits, engaging our partners in a shared purpose and then leading them toward a shared future. I recognized that many of our partners were burdened with fear. Fear of risk. Fear of public failure. And in an uncertain economy, fear for their own futures, which were tied to the future of the company....
>
> Starbucks was going to be courageous.[24]

Schultz offered reassurance that "things are going to get better." And he asked for engagement: "The power of this company is you." He and the management team then "got into the mud." They were accessible, showing up, listening to, and talking with Starbucks's partners and employees to identify inefficiencies and gather ideas for improvement, "threading optimism into every communication."[25]

Schultz said in a letter to all partners, "As we execute this transformation, there are certain integral aspects of our company that will not change at all. These include our commitment to treating each other with respect and dignity, providing health care and Bean Stock for all of our eligible full- and part-time partners, and our commitment to our community efforts, our ethical sourcing practices and encouraging our coffee suppliers to participate in our CAFE practices program in our origin countries."[26] His goal? To inspire and challenge employees to be personally accountable for everything at their stores. Ten thousand people left New Orleans with "a tidal wave of energy."

Since then Starbucks has rebounded, with strong revenue and profits, and the company is again soaring. As Schultz said in a recent interview, "When you're surrounded by people who share a passionate commitment around a common purpose, anything is possible."[27]

We can do total makeovers by engaging in deep aspirational questioning, as Starbucks did. On-site, face-to-face engagement is certainly powerful, but we can also crowdsource key stakeholders as part of a more gentle reinspiring aspiration process, such as Berrett-Koehler (BK), a San Francisco global publishing company (and publisher of this book) recently did. In an effort to reignite its brand and values and reassess its mission and key value proposition, BK surveyed online its customers, authors, employees, service providers, and other community members. The goal was to crowdsource diverse stakeholder views on how the company should evolve to keep abreast with changing technology and external demands. The great thing about stakeholder engagement, whether face-to-face or online, is that BK not only obtained innovative multiperspective input but also fostered increased dedication and commitment.

From this multistakeholder input, Berrett-Koehler forged a new mission that was grounded in the past but reflected the future: *Connecting people and ideas to create a world that works for all.* For BK this revised mission captures its belief that

> to truly create a better world, action is needed at all levels—individual, organizational, and societal. At the individual level, our books help people align their lives with their values and with their aspirations for a better world. At the organizational

level, our books promote progressive leadership and management practices, socially responsible approaches to business, and humane and effective organizations. At the societal level, our books advance social and economic justice, shared prosperity, sustainability, and new solutions to national and global issues.[28]

At Princess Margaret Cancer Centre, President and CEO Paul Alofs tried a different strategy to reinspire those in his hospital who seemed to have lost hope. He recognized that at Princess Margaret, fighting cancer could be a discouraging and seemingly endless battle for his people. He pivoted the organization from concentrating on disappointment and sorrow to optimism and advocacy.

After his mother died of cancer, Alofs realized that he could reframe the focus of the Princess Margaret by reminding people of all of its accomplishments to date, such as radical mastectomies giving way to less-invasive lumpectomies, revolutions in image-guided therapy, and advances in genetic testing for cancer. "It may seem like we'll be fighting this fight forever," Alofs wrote. "But we won't. Because we're closing in. We have the momentum. We have the talent. And we have the passion. This is the front line. We are Canada's cancer warriors. But we can't do it alone."[29] Paralleling the reframe, Princess Margaret engaged the community by organizing the Ride to Conquer Cancer, which since 2008 has raised more than $200 million. And in an act of true commitment to the larger cause, the hospital encouraged other cancer-fighting organizations to replicate its strategies across the country.

What is interesting in all three of these examples—Starbucks, Berrett-Koehler, and Princess Margaret Cancer Centre—is how essential the power of stakeholder outreach and input is for reinspiring aspirations and igniting passion with an invitation to participate in and contribute to rebuilding aspirations, hopes, and dreams.

Conclusion

Organizations that bridge the values gap successfully focus on hopes and dreams, but the emphasis is not so much on finding the perfect words but on the processes of inquiry associated with conversations about aspirations. At a fundamental level, aspirational values ask how we infuse meaning in what we do—the *How do we make a difference?* and *Why do we matter?* questions. As we see with companies like Whole Foods Market, Starbucks, Steam Whistle Brewing, O.Noir, Berrett-Koehler, and Princess Margaret Cancer Centre, aspirations not only speak to what the organization stands for but also permeate the organization and foster ongoing conversations that sustain focus on how the company believes it should contribute to the world. The stakeholder groups included and the scope of those conversations reveal a lot about the collective beliefs of an organization, how it perceives itself, and why it exists.

Thus an essential characteristic of aspirational values is that they are talked about not just in the annual report, on the company website, and at an annual retreat. Aspirational values are under continuous scrutiny and discussion, and they live and breathe in the organization through shared stories, learnings, decisions, and behavior among different stakeholder groups. Companies that excel at aspirational VTC understand that such conversations happen not just in the early development of an organization; they continue all the time, through performance declines *and* peaks, when reaspiring and inspiring may be needed. We can have the best intentions in the world, whether personal or organizational, but whether we achieve those intentions is ultimately the cumulative effect of how we live our lives, what we prioritize, where we spend our time and energy, and what choices we make and actions we take.

CONVERSATION STARTERS FOR ASPIRATIONAL VALUES

Bridging the values gap by collectively building our hopes, dreams, purpose, and how we see ourselves as contributing to our stakeholders and the greater good over time

- Is our purpose still valid?
- Why do we exist?
- What are our shared hopes and dreams?
- What do we stand for?
- What make us unique?
- How will we contribute to our organization?
- How will we contribute to our community?
- How will we make the world a better place?
- How will we measure what matters to us?
- How many lives do we positively touch?
- How is trust cultivated?
- Do our people see how their work connects to our organizational aspirations and priorities?
- How do we ensure that individual and organizational growth are aligned?
- How do we build in flexibility and choice in career paths and activities?
- How will we enable our aspirations to evolve?
- What processes do we have in place for reinspiring our aspirations?

PART III

Bringing the Conversation to Life

CHAPTER 9

Getting Started

In this final chapter, we point the way forward by offering some suggestions for how your company can be authentic, bring values conversations to life, and bridge the values gap. First, however, let us recap what we have discussed so far.

Our Main Argument

Many businesses experience a values gap. This gap is a result of several factors. Business as an institution is experiencing very low levels of trust from the public. This is due to a number of well-publicized scandals as well as the dominant belief that business is concerned only with money and profits. Even when executives want to live by a set of values, it is not easy. We do not always know what our values are, and sometimes they can conflict. Personal values can also conflict with company values. The concept that we can simply live our values, or walk the talk, is more complex than it seems.

Values are complicated. After we have engaged in some introspection about the way our lives are unfolding, they represent our desires and preferences as well as what is most important to us. Intrinsic values are our best and most thoughtful answers to *why* questions. And if we want to live a more authentic life, we must commit to an ongoing learning process. We need to be cognizant of our individual history and its influence on what is important to us. We must pay attention to our stakeholders—those groups and individuals to whom we are connected—to accomplish what we want to achieve. And we need to acknowledge our aspirations and how they can change as we progress through life.

In our organizations, we need to pay more attention to the *how* of organizational values than to their actual content, even though content is important. Organizations are joint enterprises, and if their values are to be meaningful to their members, there must be participation in bringing the values to life every day. We outlined seven critical mistakes that we have seen in our years of helping organizations think through these issues. We need to avoid these mistakes, which are subtle in difficult situations, and focus on how attention to values enables us to create even more value for our stakeholders.

There are four main aspects of the values-through-conversation process: introspective values, historical values, connectedness values, and aspirational values.

Organizations can start with a common understanding of their values, as exhibited in their behavior. There are multiple ways of devising such a statement, from IBM's widely participative Values Jam to more senior executive–driven processes, although there are shortcomings to top-down approaches, as we have highlighted.

To bring such a values statement to life, organizations must be willing to pay attention to areas that are similar to individuals' values: introspection, history, connection, and aspiration. We offer a set of questions in chapters 5 through 8 for each of these areas to help with getting these types of conversations started.

Executives can be role models by valuing reflection and introspection in their meetings. They can encourage people to experiment, to fail fast and often, and to learn from those failures. Simple techniques such as pre-mortems and after-action reviews can facilitate these ideas.

There need to be check-ins with external stakeholders to be sure that everyone is not just rationalizing what they want to happen.

Ultimately, each of these ideas of VTC must be instilled in the organization's everyday processes and systems. People can set aside time for reflection as a first step, but we need to value this reflection time and embed it in our conversations, discussions, and processes.

History is a very important part of VTC, and it must be acknowledged and discussed. In some organizations there is a tendency toward historical revisionism to fit the facts of what we want to do now. History is too often told from the standpoint of those currently in charge. Yet our history affects our *collective* identity. The stories that we tell about our history—as well as those we can imagine for our future—all constrain and enable what we are capable of doing. Through history VTC can celebrate achievements as well as yield insights for new aspirations.

Many times VTC is undertaken because of some external event that triggers the need to respond or that presents an opportunity that a company wants to proactively seize. Companies are connected to their stakeholders in whatever their chosen path for value creation. Companies cannot bridge the values gap without the support of their stakeholders in an atmosphere of trust. Sometimes this culture of trust must be declared, and sometimes it must be earned back after it has been broken. Many companies have customers who love them, who want their products and services because they improve the customers' lives. We foster thriving and more-energizing workplaces by seeing the entire set of stakeholder relationships as able to accomplish more together than alone. These relationships are intertwined, and stakeholders must be engaged in a way that honors those interconnections.

Often companies restart or revise their values conversation because a new executive team takes over who has a different and often more challenging vision of what is possible. Aspiration makes a difference. When it is not a shared aspiration, however, the values process devolves into values-talk that is often separate from real action. Aspiration is a powerful force when it is fueled by passion and brings both focus and dedication to those who share it. In our experience, aspiration and inspiration go together in companies that have closed the values gap. By making aspiration a personal issue to all employees and stakeholders, the values are more likely to be realized.

So, with that summary, let's think about three tricky problems that are often part of the values gap. Then we will offer some ideas about how we might address them using VTC.

The Values Violation Problem

A company that operated in an industry in which routine work was fraught with physical danger had a stated value of *safety first*. A new executive team took over, and though they often talked about safety, the executives were also adamant that the company meet or exceed Wall Street's earnings expectations. The previous CEO had spent a lot of time talking about values and the important role of employee development rather than focusing solely on earnings and performance. Under the new regime, employees began to take small shortcuts with respect to safety. For several years there were no big problems, and the shortcuts continued. Unfortunately, there was eventually a fatal accident that claimed the lives of several employees.

How can values through conversation ever be reinstituted in such a company?

One of the hallmarks of VTC is that we can admit our mistakes and learn from them. Given legal liabilities and the litigiousness of Western society, however, this is often difficult to do. Nonetheless there must be a reckoning about the accident. Employees and other stakeholders need to know that the company is committed to doing the right thing and to preventing future accidents.

Recall that in the wake of the *Deepwater Horizon* oil spill in the Gulf of Mexico in 2010, British Petroleum fairly quickly issued a statement that it was going to "make it right."[1] In such a difficult situation, a company could look to its history for strength. Perhaps there was an incident in the past where the company made a mistake but "made it right."

A second avenue of conversation would be to do a systems check across the company to see whether key processes were consistent with the stated values. And of course an after-action review needs to be done as well. At some point in the conversation, the acknowledgment that it was a mistake to imply that earnings were more important than safety must be made—and that this mistake was a values mistake. A fruitful conversation would uncover not only the reasons why employees thought they were getting signals that earnings were more important than safety but also what could be done to prevent such a communication breakdown in the future.

After admitting to a values violation, what is most important is that action be taken that addresses how the company will deal with the violation. Discussions about "what is really important around here" are difficult, but over time they can yield results. A conversation about a values violation needs the support of the company's top management and the participation of many levels of employees and external stakeholders.

The Derailed Values Process

A company in a competitive retail sector began a values process and had as one of its stated values *We love our customers*. The retailer passed out buttons with "We ♥ our customers." Meetings were scheduled for 7 a.m., before the stores opened, and all employees were ordered to attend, to begin the day with a rally aimed at realizing the value. Unfortunately, the company began laying off some employees while still requiring others to attend the customer rallies. The employees did not see the connection between doing a better job for their customers and the layoffs, except to see them as a contradiction that "proved" that the company was not serious about the values conversation. Needless to say, company morale was extremely low.

How would we think about values through conversation in such a derailed process?

The employees believed that the company's executives saw customers as more important than employees. Employees recognize a situation like this, often long before executives do. Addressing this problem can begin with examining the employee survey. If no such survey exists, conducting one conveys to employees that they are more important than they previously thought.

Clearly, there needs to be better introspection and communication in this company. Executives need to put themselves into the shoes of *all* of their stakeholders, not just their customers. Regardless of how important we may think our customers are, we simply cannot build a great business without the support of employees and others. There is no real tradeoff here. We must have the support of both. This company can look at its aspirations and ask, *How do we make this a great place to work, where employees want to work for us?* Once again, involving employees and other stakeholders in this process is a necessity, not an option.

Values conversations get derailed all the time. Any one of the four aspects of VTC can get them back on track. In this particular case, starting with connectedness is a good idea. The simple questions *How can we get the interests of customers and employees going in the same direction?* and *What does it feel like to be an employee [and a customer] on a daily basis here?* are great conversation starters to get things back on track.

Taking It to the Next Level

A new company in a traditional industry started with a business model that paid attention to all of its stakeholders. The company had a set of values that was unusual for the industry, and it tried very hard to live by them. The founder was still the CEO, and there was no doubt of his commitment to operating in this values-driven way. For a number of years, the company grew and was quite successful. Recently, however, the industry was undergoing a great deal of change. Although the company had long been ahead of the change curve in the industry, there was now a feeling among some employees that it was falling behind. Now that the company was much bigger than when it was in the startup phase, it was less dynamic and the values conversation was stagnant.

How can VTC be used to reenergize the company and reinvigorate the employees?

This is an extremely difficult situation in part because the founder is so committed to leading with values. The company's history is rich with good stories, and there has always been acknowledgment of connection. So, in this company and for this challenge, the levers that hold the most promise are introspection and aspiration.

Perhaps processes and systems have emerged that once reflected the values but have now atrophied. Many business executives do not understand that the processes we use today must reflect the reality of our situation, not some reality that existed when the company was started. Processes, systems, and practices are constantly being reinterpreted and recontextualized. New connections are constantly being made, just as others are being severed. There must be constant questioning about whether current practices actually reflect the values that we want to live. Beginning a conversation by revisiting the company's aspirations and linking those to the changes in the industry could be a good start. Or we could address the issue of the diminished level of reflection and introspection. If the founder is sensitive to having an honest conversation about values, the question could become, *What has happened to our conversation about our values, and how do we improve it?*

In our experience, when there is a plateau in values, absent some wake-up call from outside forces, employees inside the firm must deliver the message. Unfortunately, this message is often delivered by a key executive on his or her way out, but even those incidents are often explained away by the phrase *better opportunities elsewhere.*

Each of these real-life examples can be addressed using the tools and techniques we have developed throughout this book. None of the conversations is easy, and all require the commitment of organizational members to work together to have conversations that enable the business to fulfill its purpose and values.

Hope for the Future

Businesses can bridge the values gap, and many are engaged in doing so. We have seen more interest today in thinking about purpose and values than at any other point in recent history. Admittedly, part of this interest comes from recognizing the inadequacies of the old narrative. The global financial crisis taught us some harsh lessons about the single-minded and narrow pursuit of short-term self-interest. We want to highlight some of the reasons why we are optimistic about the future and why we believe that business is in the midst of a sea change in thinking about the future.

First, there is great energy about business models that are constructed around purposes that are greater than profits. For instance, social entrepreneurs use the power of business models to tackle difficult societal issues. They are not oriented around profits, though they must figure out a way to pay the bills on an ongoing basis and to invest in the future of their organizations. There are also facilitating organizations such as Ashoka, which supports social entrepreneurs all over the world. Many times these entrepreneurs forge partnerships with NGOs, for-profit companies, and governments. These public-private partnerships often take on issues that the individual partners could not manage on their own.

Second, there are many innovative business models that are built on understanding values. Toms Shoes has a one-for-one model whereby every pair of shoes sold triggers a donation of shoes to needy people, often in the developing world. Warby Parker has a comparable program with eyeglasses. We talked in chapter 5 about Free The Children and its sister company, Me to We, which funds its social causes. Other companies have adopted a model whereby product sales contribute to a particular charity.

Third, there is renewed interest in values-based models of business that explicitly recognize the business's social responsibility. Many large companies use their values to determine how to be better members of society and contribute more to the development of their communities. Corporate social responsibility as a business model has become the norm in many companies around the world, and many organizations have developed strategies to work collaboratively with governments, NGOs, and other players in civil society.

Fourth, companies such as Whole Foods Market and The Container Store have developed specific models of business and capitalism that are built on a purpose that is greater than profits, creating value for multiple stakeholders and leading a culture that serves all stakeholders in the organization. Under the rubric of conscious capitalism, these businesses and their founders are leading a movement to make capitalism better.[2]

Business in the twenty-first century is firmly embedded in society. We cannot focus solely on the economic costs and benefits of business or on financiers as the only legitimate beneficiary. Business today is about creating value for multiple stakeholders, and the only way to build a great business that does that is to take values seriously. The values gap must be bridged. And if we are to invent a version of capitalism that is fit for twenty-first-century human beings, it is a necessity.

We close with the simple idea that living a more authentic life inside and outside our organizations is a journey, one that is best traveled with the companions of humility, humor, and grace. Thankfully, none of us has to stand alone. If we can reach out to one another and have better conversations about what is important to us, we are more likely to lead the rich and fulfilling lives that are possible—and we are more likely to build great companies that will make the world a better place for our children.

Notes

CHAPTER 1

The Values Gap in Business

1. Erin Davies, "Enron: The Power's Back On," *Fortune*, April 13, 1998, 24–28, http://archive.fortune.com/magazines/fortune/fortune_archive /1998/04/13/240841/index.htm.

2. Rebecca Riffkin, "Public Faith in Congress Falls Again, Hits Historic Low," Gallup survey June 5–8, 2014, http://www.gallup.com/poll/171710 /public-faith-congress-falls-again-hits-historic-low.aspx.

3. Of course this is more complicated than we make it here.

4. "State of the American Workplace," Gallup report 2010–2012, www.gallup .com/services/178514/state-american-workplace.aspx.

5. Ibid.

6. See especially the work of Jim Collins and Jerry I. Porras, *Built to Last: Successful Habits of Visionary Companies*, 3rd ed. (New York: HarperCollins, 2011); and Jim Collins, *Good to Great: Why Some Companies Make the Leap...and Others Don't* (New York: HarperCollins, 2001).

CHAPTER 2

Just Be Authentic: Not So Fast, Not So Easy

1. Bill George, *Authentic Leadership: Rediscovering the Secrets to Creating Lasting Value* (San Francisco: Jossey-Bass, 2003).

2. William Shakespeare, *Hamlet, Prince of Denmark,* act 1, sc. 3, edited by K. Deighton (London: Macmillan, 1919), Shakespeare Online, accessed February 12, 2015. http://www.shakespeare-online.com/plays/hamlet_1_3 .html.

3. Daniel Kahneman, *Thinking Fast and Slow* (New York: Farrar, Straus and Giroux, 2011).

4. Edwin Hartman, *Conceptual Foundations of Organization Theory* (Pensacola, FL: Ballinger, 1988), 75.

5. Donald Davidson, *The Essential Davidson* (New York: Oxford University Press, 2006).

6. See Hans Joas, *The Genesis of Values* (Chicago: University of Chicago Press, 2000); Charles Taylor, *The Ethics of Authenticity* (Cambridge, MA: Harvard University Press, 1991); and Kevin T. Jackson, "Towards Authenticity: A Sartrean Perspective on Business Ethics," *Journal of Business Ethics* 58, no. 4 (2005): 307–25.

7. Mollie Painter-Morland, *Business Ethics as Practice: Ethics as the Everyday Business of Business* (New York: Cambridge University Press, 2008).

CHAPTER **3**

Authentic Organizations: Is Yours One?

1. For an analysis of how DuPont thinks about safety, see Thomas J. Peters and Robert H. Waterman Jr., *In Search of Excellence: Lessons from America's Best-Run Companies* (New York: HarperCollins, 1982).

2. See David Wheeler and Maria Sillanpaa, *The Stakeholder Corporation* (Upper Saddle River, NJ: FT Press, 1997).

3. For the Nokia story, see Anton Troianovski and Sven Grundberg, "Nokia's Bad Call on Smartphones," *Wall Street Journal*, July 18, 2012, http://online .wsj.com/news/articles/SB10001424052702304388004577531002591315494; and Tomi T. Ahonen, "Undesirable at Any Price? What Happened to Nokia, Who Invented the Smartphone" (blog), January 27, 2011, http://communities-dominate.blogs.com/brands/2011/01/undesirable-at -any-price-what-happened-to-Nokia-who-invented-the-smartphone .html.

4. Personal correspondence with research associate Sergiy Dmytriyev, September 30, 2014.

5. "Our Vision," Unilever, accessed February 17, 2015, http://www.unilever .com/aboutus/introductiontounilever/ourmission.

6. See the interview by R. Edward Freeman with John Mackey, "What Is the Purpose of Business?" University of Virginia Darden School of Business, January 12, 2011, https://www.youtube.com/watch?v=6ncsJGxkZdQ& index=2&list=PL43B5DF2B45A8B49C.

7. "About The Motley Fool," The Motley Fool, accessed February 17, 2015, https://www.fool.com/press/about-the-motley-fool.aspx#purpose.

8. See the interview by R. Edward Freeman with Tom Gardner, "Conscious Capitalism and CEO Tom Gardner of The Motley Fool," University of Virginia Darden School of Business, March 26, 2013, https://www.youtube .com/watch?v=WJUQLllKQBs.

CHAPTER **4**

Do Values Right or Don't Do Them at All

1. Stanley Milgram, *Obedience to Authority: An Experimental View* (New York: Harper & Row, 1974).

2. James Burke's view is from a television program, *Business Ethics Round-table,* produced by WVET in New York in 1992.

3. Jim Collins and Jerry I. Porras, *Built to Last: Successful Habits of Visionary Companies*, 3rd ed. (New York: HarperCollins, 2011).

4. Anne Mäkikangas, Taru Felt, Ulla Kinnunen, and Asko Tolvanen, "Do Low Burnout and High Work Engagement Always Go Hand in Hand? Investigation of the Energy and Identification Dimensions in Longitudinal Data," *Anxiety, Stress, and Coping* 25, no. 1 (2012): 93–116, doi: 10.1080/10615806.2011.565411. Also see J. Lee Whittington and Timothy J. Galpin, "The Engagement Factor: Building a High-Commitment Organization in a Low-Commitment World," *Journal of Business Strategy* 31, no. 5 (2010): 14–24, doi: 10.1108/02756661011076282.

CHAPTER **5**

Introspective Values:
Reflecting on Self and the Organization

1. Max H. Bazerman and Ann E. Tenbrunsel, *Blind Spots: Why We Fail to Do What's Right and What to Do about It* (Princeton, NJ: Princeton University Press, 2011).

2. Susan Scott, "The Case for Radical Transparency," TED Overlake video published June 30, 2011, http://www.youtube.com/watch?v=oVKaXUB4EFg.

3. Nate Boaz and Erica Ariel Fox, "Change Leader, Change Thyself," *McKinsey Quarterly*, March 2014, http://www.mckinsey.com/insights/leading_in _the_21st_century/change_leader_change_thyself.

4. Graham Allison and Philip Zelikow, *Essence of Decision: Explaining the Cuban Missile Crisis* (New York: Longman, 1999).

5. Chris Hadfield, *An Astronaut's Guide to Life: What Going to Space Taught Me about Ingenuity, Determination, and Being Prepared for Anything* (New York: Little, Brown, 2013).

6. See George C. Halvorson, "The Culture to Cultivate," *Harvard Business Review*, July 2013, 34, https://hbr.org/2013/07/the-culture-to-cultivate; and Jayne O'Donnell, "The Kaiser Way: Lesson for U.S. Health Care?" *USA Today*, http://www.usatoday.com/story/news/nation/2014/08/06 /kaiser-permanente-obamacare-accountable-care-organizations -hospitals/12763591.

7. See "Kaiser Permanente MedRite Program," Institute for Healthcare Improvement, accessed February 11, 2015, http://www.ihi.org/resources /Pages/Tools/KPMedRiteProgram.aspx.

8. See more at "About Kaiser Permanente," accessed February 11, 2015, http: //share.kaiserpermanente.org/about-kaiser-permanente/#sthash .1HChBscy.dpuf.

9. See "Schlumberger Cited for Knowledge Management," accessed February 11, 2015, http://www.slb.com/news/inside_news/2010/2010_0312 _make_award.aspx.

10. Amy C. Edmondson, *Teaming to Innovate* (San Francisco: Jossey-Bass, 2013).

11. Michael Jordan, "Failure," accessed February 11, 2015, https://www.youtube .com/watch?v=GuXZFQKKF7A.

12. "Next Time, What Say We Boil a Consultant," *Fast Company*, accessed February 11, 2015, http://www.fastcompany.com/26455/next-time-what -say-we-boil-consultant.

13. Tim Bajarin, "6 Reasons Why Apple Is So Successful," *Time,* May 7, 2012, http://techland.time.com/2012/05/07/six-reasons-why-apple-is -successful; and Michael Pascoe, "What to Learn from Sony's Greatest Mistake," *Sydney Morning Herald,* June 28, 2010, http://www.smh.com .au/business/what-to-learn-from-sonys-greatest-mistake-20120628-21405 .html.

14. George Gendron, "The Entrepreneur of the Decade," *Inc.,* April 1, 1989, http://www.inc.com/magazine/19890401/5602.html.

15. Jason Snell, "Steve Jobs on the Mac's 20th Anniversary," *Macworld,* February 2, 2004, http://www.macworld.com/article/1029181/themac turns20jobs.html.

16. Richard J. Leider and Alan M. Webber, *Life Reimagined: Discovering Your New Life Possibilities* (San Francisco: Berrett-Koehler, 2013), 72–75.

17. See "Our Values at Work," IBM Corporation, accessed February 25, 2015, http://www.ibm.com/ibm/values/us.

18. See Barclays case study, IBM Corporation, accessed February 25, 2015, http://www-03.ibm.com/software/businesscasestudies/us/en /corp?synkey=L637183D14221K13.

19. See "My Starbucks Idea," Starbucks Corporation, accessed February 25, 2015, http://mystarbucksidea.force.com.

20. See "Our Core Values," Free The Children, accessed February 25, 2015, http://www.freethechildren.com/about-us/our-core-values.

21. See "Our Mission and Our Model," Free The Children, accessed February 25, 2015, http://www.freethechildren.com/about-us/our-model.

22. See "Our Organization," Me to We, accessed February 11, 2015, http://www .metowe.com/about-us/our-organization.

23. See We Day home page, Free The Children, accessed February 11, 2015, http://www.weday.com.

CHAPTER **6**

Historical Values: Exploring the Impact of Our Past

1. AJ Willingham, "September 11: A Virtual Memorial," HLN TV, September 11, 2012, http://www.hlntv.com/slideshow/2012/09/11/911-september -11th-memorial-photos.

2. William H. McNeill, "Why Study History?" American Historical Association, http://www.historians.org/about-aha-and-membership/aha-history -and-archives/archives/why-study-history-(1985).

3. Lonnie R. Sherrod, ed., *Youth Activism: An International Encyclopedia*, vol. 1 (Westport, CT: Greenwood, 2006), 119.

4. Craig Kielburger, Free the Children by Me to We (personal appearance), Toronto, 2011; and Trish Ruebottom, "The Role of Story in Institutional Work" (PhD thesis, Schulich School of Business, York University, May 2013).

5. For further reading see Alex Davies, "Unbelievable Photos from Lamborghini's Birthday Tour of Italy," *Business Insider,* May 15, 2013, http://www.businessinsider.com/lamborghinis-crazy-50th-anniversary-tour -2013-5?op=1#ixzz3RSzOzzQu.

6. Tony Hsieh, "Your Culture Is Your Brand," Huffington Post, November 15, 2010, http://www.huffingtonpost.com/tony-hsieh/zappos-founder-tony -hsieh_1_b_783333.html.

7. Paul Simpson, "M&A: How to Create Value, Not Headlines," *Agenda,* April/May 2011, 10, http://paperzz.com/doc/1503902/%E2%80%9C-india -has-showed-the-world-how-to-manage-an-economy---kpmg.

8. John T. Seaman Jr. and George David Smith, "Your Company's History as a Leadership Tool," *Harvard Business Review* 90, no. 12 (2012): 46, https://hbr.org/2012/12/your-companys-history-as-a-leadership-tool.

9. Ibid., 44–52.

10. Gary W. Loveman, Leonard A. Schlesinger, and Robert T. Anthony, "Euro Disney: The First 100 Days," *Harvard Business Review* case study #693013 (1992), https://hbr.org/product/Euro-Disney--The-First-10/an/693013 -PDF-ENG.

11. "All-Time Box-Office Top 100 Films [through December 2014]," American Movie Classics Company, http://www.filmsite.org/boxoffice.html.

12. "21 McDonald's Meals You Won't Find in America," Huffington Post, January 20, 2013, http://www.huffingtonpost.com/2013/01/19/mcdonalds -international-menu_n_2507006.html; "30 Crazy Meals from McDonald's Menus around the World," Food Network, accessed March 13, 2015, http: //www.foodnetwork.co.uk/article/crazy-meals-mcdonalds-menus -around-world.html; Susan L. Nasr, "10 Unusual Items from McDonald's International Menu," How Stuff Works, accessed March 13, 2015, http: //money.howstuffworks.com/10-items-from-mcdonalds-international -menu.htm#page=5; and "Discover McDonald's around the Globe," McDonald's Corporation, accessed March 13, 2015, http://www.about mcdonalds.com/mcd/country/map.html.

13. Paul Alofs, *Passion Capital: The World's Most Valuable Asset* (Toronto: McClelland & Stewart, 2012), 23.

CHAPTER **7**

Connectedness Values:
Creating a Sense of Belonging and Community

1. Jeffrey Herbst, "Message from President Herbst," *Scene*, Autumn 2014, 3, http://news.colgate.edu/scene/2014/11/message-from-president-herbst-2 .html.

2. "Update on Campus-Climate Demonstration in James B. Colgate Hall," Colgate News, September 22, 2014, http://www.colgate.edu/about/people -of-colgate/president-jeffrey-herbst/colgate-for-all/messages-and -updates.

3. "September 23 Update on Campus-Climate Demonstration," Colgate News, September 23, 2014, http://news.colgate.edu/2014/09/september -23-update-on-campus-climate-demonstration.html; and "Chapel Bell Tolls 13 Times to Mark End of 100-Hour-Long Demonstration," Colgate News, September 23, 2014, http://news.colgate.edu/2014/09/chapel-bell -tolls-13-times-to-mark-end-of-100-hour-long-demonstration.html.

4. "Peaceful Demonstration Concludes with Release of 21-Point Road Map," Colgate News, September 26, 2014, http://www.colgate.edu/about/people

-of-colgate/president-jeffrey-herbst/colgate-for-all/messages-and -updates.

5. See Maia Szalavitz, "Social Isolation, Not Just Feeling Lonely, May Shorten Lives," *Time,* March 26, 2013, http://healthland.time.com/2013/03/26 /social-isolation-not-just-feeling-lonely-may-shorten-lives; and Alice Park, "How Feeling Lonely Can Shorten Your Life," *Time,* June 19, 2012, http://healthland.time.com/2012/06/19/how-feeling-lonely-can-shorten -your-life.

6. Beebe Bahrami, "Finding an Old Flame," *Pennsylvania Gazette,* January 8, 2014, http://thepenngazette.com/finding-an-old-flame.

7. Michael Tomasello, *Why We Cooperate* (Cambridge, MA: MIT Press, 2009).

8. Howard Schultz with Joanne Gordon, *Onward: How Starbucks Fought for Its Life without Losing Its Soul* (New York: Rodale, 2011), 117.

9. David Elsner (general manager of The Global Group of Companies), in discussion with the authors, November 2014.

10. David Novak with John Boswell, *The Education of an Accidental CEO: Lessons Learned from the Trailer Park to the Corner Office* (New York: Three Rivers Press, 2007).

11. See the interview by Jennifer Reingold with Christine Day, "How to Turn Your Customers into a Community," *Fortune,* November 26, 2012, http: //www.youtube.com/watch?v=XR6HSpLjO8g.

12. Ibid.

13. For further reading see Emily Wexler, "Brands of the Year: Lululemon Takes Local to the Next Level," Strategy Online, September 28, 2012, http: //strategyonline.ca/2012/09/28/brands-of-the-year-lululemon-takes-local -to-the-next-level/#ixzz3RTCFmisS.

14. "Ratan Tata's Humane Gestures (in the aftermath of 26/11)," Rotary Club of Bombay, accessed February 11, 2015, http://rotaryclubofbombay.org/Article .aspx?articleid=13738fa7-8dbd-4a8f-935e-4717a2d86d48&cid=b4cf3f4b -a832-4287-afe6-c484d37f2dab; and Cynthia Rodrigues, "Taj Public Service Welfare Trust," Tata Sons, February 2010, http://www.tata.com/article /inside/pSHrq3pPRBQ=/TLYVr3YPkMU=.

15. Richard Zitrin, "A Lethal Culture of Secrecy at G.M.," letter to the editor, *New York Times,* June 10, 2014, http://mobile.nytimes.com/2014/06/11 /opinion/a-lethal-culture-of-secrecy-at-gm.html.

16. Anne Vandermey, "Whitewater Rafting? 12 Unusual Perks," *Fortune,* January 20, 2012, http://archive.fortune.com/galleries/2012/pf/jobs/1201 /gallery.best-companies-unusual-perks.fortune/3.html.

17. Course feedback, SGMT 6700, Schulich School of Business, winter 2014 and 2015.

18. Steve Hamm, "A Passion for the Planet," Bloomberg Business, August 20, 2006, http://www.bloomberg.com/bw/stories/2006-08-20/a-passion-for -the-planet.

19. Adele Diamond, "The Evidence Base for Improving School Outcomes by Addressing the Whole Child and by Addressing Skills and Attitudes, Not Just Content," *Early Education and Development* 21, no. 5 (2010): 780–93, doi: 10.1080/10409289.2010.514522.

20. Douglas A. Ready, Linda Hill, and Robert J. Thomas, "Building a Game-Changing Talent Strategy," *Harvard Business Review,* January 2014, 62–67, https://hbr.org/2014/01/building-a-game-changing-talent-strategy.

21. "The Case Against Layoffs: They Often Backfire," *Newsweek,* February 4, 2010, http://www.newsweek.com/case-against-layoffs-they-often-backfire -75039.

22. Nancy Messieh, "12 Tech Companies That Offer Their Employees the Coolest Perks," The Next Web (blog), April 9, 2012, http://thenextweb.com /insider/2012/04/09/12-startups-that-offer-their-employees-the-coolest -perks.

CHAPTER **8**

Aspirational Values: Our Hopes and Dreams

1. Carl Sandburg, "Washington Monument by Night," stanza 4, *The Complete Poems of Carl Sandburg,* revised and expanded ed. (Orlando, FL: Harcourt, Brace, 1970), 282.

2. Lisa Hillenbrand (director of global marketing at Procter & Gamble), in discussion with the authors, November 1, 2012.

3. Towers Watson 2012 Global Workforce Study: *Engagement at Risk: Driving Strong Performance in a Volatile Global Environment*, July 2012, www.towerswatson.com/Insights/IC-Types/Survey-Research-Results/2012/07/2012-Towers-Watson-Global-Workforce-Study.

4. For example, see Robert Biswas-Diener and Todd B. Kashdan, "What Happy People Do Differently," *Psychology Today*, June 19, 2014, https://www.psychologytoday.com/articles/201306/what-happy-people-do-differently; Melanie Rudd, Jennifer Aaker, and Michael I. Norton, "Getting the Most Out of Giving: Concretely Framing a Prosocial Goal Maximizes Happiness," *Journal of Experimental Social Psychology* 54 (September 2014): 11–24, doi: 10.1016/j.jesp.2014.04.002; and Cecile K. Cho and Gita Venkataramani Johar, "Attaining Satisfaction," *Journal of Consumer Research* 38, no. 4 (2011): 622–31, http://www.jstor.org/stable/10.1086/660115.

5. R. Edward Freeman, "Business Is about Purpose," TED Charlottesville video published January 25, 2014, https://www.youtube.com/watch?v=7dugfwJthBY.

6. Rajendra S. Sisodia, David B. Wolfe, and Jagdish N. Sheth, *Firms of Endearment: How World-Class Companies Profit from Passion and Purpose*, 2nd ed. (Upper Saddle River, NJ: Pearson Education, 2014).

7. Robert Musslewhite, "How Companies Can Profit from Doing Good," *Fast Company*, June 20, 2014, http://www.fastcompany.com/3032059/bottom-line/how-companies-can-profit-from-doing-good.

8. Paul Alofs, *Passion Capital: The World's Most Valuable Asset* (Toronto: McClelland & Stewart, 2012), 19.

9. See "Declaration of Interdependence," Whole Foods, accessed February 11, 2015, http://www.wholefoodsmarket.com/company/declaration.php.

10. US Environmental Protection Agency, Green Power Partnership report, July 2013, http://www.epa.gov/greenpower/toplists/partner100.htm.

11. Jim Dobson, "Blind Date: Adventure Dining in the Dark at Canada's Popular O.Noir Restaurant," *Forbes*, September 20, 2014, http://www.forbes.com/sites/jimdobson/2014/09/20/blind-date-adventure-dining-in-the-dark-at-canadas-popular-o-noir-restaurant.

12. Jim Goodnight, "Chief Executive Officer, SAS," accessed March 3, 2015, http://www.sas.com/en_sg/company-information/executive-bios/jim -goodnight.html.

13. Mark C. Crowley, "How SAS Became the World's Best Place to Work," *Fast Company,* January 22, 2013, http://www.fastcompany.com/3004953 /how-sas-became-worlds-best-place-work.

14. Howard Schultz, interview by Jon Stewart, *The Daily Show,* Comedy Central, June 16, 2014, http://thedailyshow.cc.com/videos/4lqlz1/howard -schultz.

15. "Starbucks Offers Workers 2 Years of Free College," CNN Money, June 16, 2014, http://money.cnn.com/2014/06/15/news/economy /starbucks-schultz-education.

16. See "Vision and Goals," Luluemon, accessed February 11, 2015, http://www .lululemon.com/education/goalsetting. Also see Michael Tushman, "Leadership, Culture, and Transition at Lululemon," *Harvard Business Review* case study #410705 (2010), https://hbr.org/product/leadership-culture -and-transition-at-lululemon-multimedia-case/410705-MMC-ENG.

17. Howard Schultz with Joanne Gordon, *Onward: How Starbucks Fought for Its Life without Losing Its Soul* (New York: Rodale, 2011), 9-13. Also see "Why Starbucks CEO Howard Schultz Says Leaders Should Be Vulnerable," *Oprah* video (season 4, episode 435, aired on December 8, 2013), http://www.oprah.com/own-super-soul-sunday/Starbucks-CEO-Howard -Schultz-Says-Leaders-Should-Be-Vulnerable-Video.

18. Schultz, *Onward,* 153.

19. "Text of Starbucks Memo," *Wall Street Journal,* February 14, 2007; text available at Starbucks Gossip, accessed February 11, 2015, http://starbucks gossip.typepad.com/_/2007/02/starbucks_chair_2.html.

20. Schultz, *Onward,* 193.

21. Ibid., 195.

22. Ibid., 241.

23. Ibid., 75.

24. Ibid., 254.

25. Ibid., 98–99.

26. "Howard Schultz Transformation Agenda Communication #1," Starbucks Newsroom, January 6, 2008, http://news.starbucks.com/news/howard -schultz-transformation-agenda-communication-1.

27. "Why Starbucks CEO Howard Schultz Says Leaders Should Be Vulnerable," Oprah video.

28. See "About Berrett-Koehler Publishers," Berrett-Koehler, accessed February 11, 2015, https://www.bkconnection.com/home/bk-community-menu /about-berrett-koehler-publishers?redirected=true.

29. Princess Margaret Hospital Foundation, "2009: Report to Our Donors," http: //www.thepmcf.ca/pmcf/pmcf/Our%20Impact/2009/2009AnnualReport .pdf.

CHAPTER **9**
Getting Started

1. Whether British Petroleum actually delivered on its promise is a subject of debate; but if the company had not made the verbal commitment, it would have had even less credibility with its employees and other stakeholders.

2. See http://www.consciouscapitalism.org; and John Mackey and Raj Sisodia, *Conscious Capitalism* (Cambridge, MA: Harvard Business Review Press), 2013.

Index

absenteeism, 140

activities for building community, 125–126

adaptation, 51, 104, 106, 108, 109

after-action reviews (AARs), 74

ahistorical operation, 93

Alameddine, Moe, 146

Alofs, Paul, 108

animal testing, 34, 36–37

An Inconvenient Truth (Gore), 80–81

anthropological dives, 73–74, 82

AOL, 77, 104

Apple, 34, 35, 81

appreciations before meetings, 74

Aristotle, 19

Arm & Hammer, 82

Arthur Andersen, 4

Ashoka, 166

aspirational values, 63
   benefits of, 139–142
   bridging personal and organizational growth, 147–148
   bridging the values gap with, 138, 141–153
   conversation starters for, 155
   "do good, do better," 142–147
   for infusing meaning, 154
   meaningful aspirations, 139
   reinspiring aspiration and purpose, 148–153
   role in values through conversation of, 137–139

aspirations, 57, 148–153, 150–151, 161–162, 165

assumptions
   challenging, 119
   mistaken, 105–106

authenticity/authentic life
   committing to learning process, 159–160
   conflicting values and, 9
   conversations about values for, 44–45
   difficulties of/for, 32–37
   growth and development of, 39
   importance of, 127
   as journey, 167–168
   lack of authenticity, 31
   meaning of, 17–18
   problem of, 18
   as process (examples), 26–29
   process of, 58–59

Authentic Leadership (George), 17

authority position, leading by, 61–62

authority system, 35

autonomy, 25–26

balance, work/life, 36, 132–133

balanced scorecard initiatives, 129

Barclays, 85–86

Bebo, 77

beginner's mind (*shoshin*), 69, 85

behavior
   deducing values from, 18–19
   drivers of, 22
   as example, 57
   feedback on, 20
   values exhibited in, 160

belief systems
   acting/not acting on, 20, 37
   importance of values, 9–12

Berrett-Koehler (BK), 152–153

Best Buy, 82

better together connectedness value, 118–124

"better to not get into it" mistake,
  51–52
BlackRock, 127
blameworthy failure, 77
blind spots, 69
Body Shop, The, 34, 36–37
boiling-frog analogy, 79–80, 83, 89, 94
Boston Consulting Group, 79
branding, 7, 152
brand values, 121
British Petroleum (BP), 162–163
building community, 125
"built to last" companies, 58
Burke, James E., 55–56
Bush, George W., 5
businesses
  history of (*See* history of the
    organization)
  as human institution, 14–15
  in twenty-first century, 6–8
business ethics, 54
"business is great" stories, 6
business models
  activation of business strategy, 56
  connecting values to, 55–58
  conscious capitalism, 167
  discipline, efficiency, innovation,
    58
  empowerment and engagement of
    employees, 55–56
  ethics and values in, 13, 54
  innovative, 166–167
  reasons for connecting values to, 55
  social, 166
  value creation, 57
  values-based, 58, 167
  vision and purpose, 57

Cadbury, John, 104–105
Cadbury/Kraft Foods merger, 104–105
CALL (Center for Army Lessons
    Learned), 74
Camus, Albert, 91
capitalism, 14, 167

celebrations
  accomplishments/milestones, 92,
    98, 124, 161
  anniversaries, 96, 101, 107
  creating collective narrative
    through, 103, 110
  need for, 6
  successes, 61
  We Day, 88, 100
Center for Army Lessons Learned
    (CALL), 74
change
  effecting positive, 100
  in life direction (examples), 26–29
  strategic, 125
  triggers for, 85
  unchanging values, 58
changing values, 20–21, 35
Chazan, Michael, 116
child labor, 7
choice, leading by, 61–62
choices, 91
Colgate University, 111, 113–114, 127
collective history, 99–103, 103–104
Collins, Jim, 58
commitment
  as value, 87
  to values, 85
common ground, 113
communication about values. *See* con-
    versations about values
community-building strategies, 125
competing values, 53–54
conflict about values, 3–4, 19, 22–23
conflicting values, 8–9, 50, 53–54, 58
conflict resolution, 60–61
connectedness values, 63
  being one's whole self, 131–133
  benefits of relationships, 133–134
  better together/sense of "we,"
    118–124
  bridging the values gap with, 112,
    118–133
  Colgate University sit-in, 111,
    113–114, 127

conversation starters for, 135
problems of missing, 115–116
relational work, 124–131
role in values through conversation of, 114–117
connections/connectedness, 165
benefits of, 117–118
through values, 25
See also relationships
conscious capitalism, 167
Container Store, The, 74
content of values, 38
context
changing, 108–109
of creative, authentic life, 38–39
paying attention to, 79–80
of values, 21–22, 24
conversations (in general)
about history of the organization, 95, 106
employees involvement in, 59
safety conversation example, 162
with stakeholders, 83, 108
conversations about values, 32–33
aspirational, 154, 155
for authenticity/authentic life, 44–45
conflicts between personal and company values, 51–52
connectedness, 114
emergence of values through, 38–39
with employees, 51
ideas for starting, 90, 110, 135, 155
lack of honest, 54
mistakes of, 62
one-way, 52–53
overcoming problems through, 58–62
reinvigorating company/employees through, 165–166
roles of senior executives and entrepreneurs, 42–44
starting, 39–44
values statements as drivers of, 41
See also values through conversation (VTC)

conversation starters
aspirational values, 155
connectedness values, 135
historical values, 110
introspective values, 90
values, 39–44
cooperators, 117
core values. *See* values statements
cost containment, 43, 128, 130
cover-ups, 123
creativity, 43
credibility, 32
crisis management, 96, 122–123
criticism, 60
Cromwell, Greg, 145–146
crowdsourcing, 85–86
Cuban Missile Crisis, 72
cultural differences, 106
culture of company, 143, 144
dysfunctional, 37–38
innovation as, 35
relevance of values to, 44
customers
anthropological dives with, 82
feedback from, 73–74, 82
ideas generated by, 86
interests of, 164
learning from, 108
cycles/patterns, 98–99, 132

Dallimore, Lesia, 121
Davidson, Donald, 22
Day, Christine, 121
Day of Giving, 122
decision making, 91, 95
derailed values process, 163–164
Diamond, Adele, 126
dichotomies, profit/return, 12–13
discipline, 58
Disney Corporation, 102–107
disruptions, management's response to, 7
dissent, 127–128

"do good, do better" aspiration, 142–147

Drucker, Peter, 56

DuPont, 34

eBay, 104

Edmonson, Amy, 77–78

efficiency, 58

Elsner, David, 119–120

emotional connections, 118, 131

employees
  activating, 57
  aspirations of, 143
  as assets, 37–38, 115, 147
  benefits for, 148
  commitment/loyalty to, 122
  conflicts between personal and
    company values, 51–52
  empowerment and engagement of,
    55–56
  engagement of, 10–11, 119, 140,
    151–152
  getting feedback from, 71
  incentives for, 129
  inspiring/challenging, 152
  interests of, 164
  invested, 120
  investing in, 148
  invisible, 123
  involvement in conversations, 59
  layoff alternatives, 128–130
  morale, 163–164
  motivating, 43
  Motley values of, 44
  reaching out to, 126–127
  recognition programs, 123
  reinvigorating, 165–166
  salaries/bonuses, 145
  values as shield for, 56
  values violations, 163
  view of values by, 50–51
  work/life balance, 36, 132–133

empowerment, 9–12, 55–56, 100

empty values, 37–39, 41

engagement
  asking for, 151

studies on employee, 10–11
  through values, 55–56

engaging our values, 29

Enron, 4, 140

entrepreneurs, 13, 42–44

environment, supportive, 117, 125

Environmental Protection Agency, 145

ethical businesses, 5–6

ethical issues
  in business models, 54, 152
  lack of ethics, 5
  learning and valuing ethics, 21
  policy exceptions, 4
  teaching, 13
  unethical practices, 140
  valuing ethics/integrity, 53
  views of business ethics, 3, 8

everyday processes
  embedding introspection into,
    72–79
  introspection, 76–77, 79

evolution
  human, 116, 117
  organizational, 103–108, 108–109
  of purpose, 92
  of self and ideas, 24–25
  vision statements, 149

executives. *See* leaders/leadership

expectations, 57, 85

extrinsic rewards, 33

extrinsic values, 22

failures, 77
  learning from, 98
  reasons for, 105–106
  recast as successes, 78

false dichotomy, 12–13

family, 132–133

Fast Company, 79, 84, 147

feedback, 49, 50
  asking employees for, 60, 71
  on behavior, 20
  customer, 73–74, 82
  from stakeholders, 71, 152

focus groups, 74

foolishness, as core value, 43–44

forcing values, 37

Ford, Rob, 123

Fortune magazine, America's Most Innovative Company award, 4

founding stories, 100

fraud, 4, 5

Free The Children (FTC), 86–88, 99–101, 167

frog experiment analogy, 79–80, 83, 89, 94

future orientation
    ahistorical operation, 93
    macro trends, 80
    new narratives for business, 12–15
    problems of, 68–69
    tendency for, 61
    values and engagement, 11–12

Gardner, Tom, 43–44

Gates, Bill, 42

General Motors, 123

George, Bill, 17

Giuliani, Rudy, 97–98

give-back initiatives, 121–122

Global Group of Companies, 119–120

globalization, 6–7

glocalization, 107–108

goals
    alignment of personal and organizational, 142
    aspirational, 140, 147
    conflicting, 53
    connecting through, 115, 120
    focusing on/realizing, 68–69
    importance of, 148
    introspection for reaching, 90
    shared, 42, 113

good cooperators, 117

Goodnight, Jim, 147

Google, 147

Gore, Al, 80–81

Gotham Greens Farms, 144–145

Great Place to Work Institute, 147

growth, 147–148

habits/routines, 72

Hadfield, Chris, 73

Halverson, George, 75

Hamlet, 17–18

happiness, 140–141

Harley-Davidson, 74

Hartman, Edwin, 19–20

"head, heart, and hands" check-ins, 131

Heaps, Cam, 145–146

Herbst, Jeffrey, 111, 113–114

Hero Award, 123

historical values, 63
    bridging the values gap with, 92, 95–108
    conversation starters for, 110
    focus of, 93

history of the organization
    ahistorical approach, 93
    anchoring aspirations in, 149
    benefits of understanding the, 93–95
    conversations about, 95, 106
    conversation starters, 110
    creating a collective, 99–103
    differing views of, 94
    founding stories, 100–101
    gratitude for the journey, 96–98
    honoring legacy, embracing evolution, 103–108
    importance of, 91, 109
    making mistakes right, 162–163
    role in values through conversation of, 91–93

Honda, 102

hope for the future, 166–168

human evolution, 116, 117

Husk Power Systems, 57

hypocrisy, 20, 47

IBM, 85

idea generation, 127–128

idea of self, 23–26

identifying our values, 25

identity
  collective, 118–124, 161
  understanding, 103–104

IDEO, 102

IKEA, 103

inclusive language, 113–114

individual/personal values, 34, 58, 160

injustices, 38

innovation consultancy, 75

innovations, 58
  as culture, 35
  unexpected, 78
  Whole Foods Market, 144–145

insights
  breakthrough, 70
  exercises for, 103
  external, 81
  leveraging, 74
  into our motivations, 20
  sources of, 19, 72, 73, 79, 82, 95, 109,
    161
  through introspection, 77, 89
  through outside-in perspective, 83
  through reflection, 22

integration of work and life, 54

integrity, 5, 49

intentionality, acting on values with,
  57

interpreting values, 18–19

InTouch, 76

intrinsic rewards, 33

intrinsic value, 22

introspection, 20, 27
  benefits of, 70–71, 75, 78, 165
  bridging the values gap with, 68,
    71–89
  embedding, into everyday
    processes, 72–79
  everyday, 76–77, 79
  leveraging, 99
  need for, 164
  as ongoing journey, 83–89
  outward, 79–83

role in values through conversation
  of, 67–70
  See also reflection

introspective values, 63, 68, 69, 71–72,
  74, 90

invisible employees, 123

inward/internal introspection, 83–84,
  85–86

Jobs, Steve, 81

Johnson & Johnson, 55–56

Jordan, Michael, 78

"just walk the talk" mistake, 48–50

Kaiser Permanente (KP), 74–76

Kapito, Robert, 127

KFC, 120

Kielburger, Craig, 87–88, 99–100

Kielburger, Marc, 87

Kraft, James L., 104–105

Kraft Foods, 104–105

Lamborghini, 96, 101–102

language of values, 49–50, 113–114,
  131–132

layoffs, 128–130, 163–164

leaders/leadership
  creation of positive environment,
    117
  leadership skills of executives, 62
  mistakes (*See* mistakes about
    values)
  mistrust in, 3, 4–6
  from position versus choice, 61–62
  questions for determining your
    business, 56
  reaching out to employees, 126–127
  as role models, 160
  roles of senior, 42–44
  shared leadership, 127
  unconventional, 150
  values-based leadership, 58

legacies, organizational, 103–108, 109

Leider, Richard, 84

life cycles, 132

life/work balance, 36, 132–133, 147
L'Oréal Group, The, 36–37
loyalty, to workforce, 6
Lululemon Athletica, 120–121, 148

Mackey, John, 42–43, 142, 143–144
macro trends, 80
market surveys, 82
M&As (mergers and acquisitions), 40, 95, 104
Massachusetts Institute of Technology (MIT), 79
McDonald's, 107–108
McKinsey study, 71
McNeill, William, 99
media, 5, 6
memories, collective, 99, 103–104
    See also history of the organization
Mentor Moms program, 132
Merck, 143
mergers and acquisitions (M&As), 40, 95, 104
Me to We, 88, 167
Microsoft, 34, 96, 103
Milgram, Stanley, 48–49
mind-set, 139–140
mission/mission statements, 76, 93, 113, 149, 150, 152–153
mistakes
    admitting/learning from, 162–163
    avoiding, 160
    mistaken assumptions, 105–106
    responding to, 84
mistakes about values, 47–48
    "better to not get into it" mistake, 51–52
    "just walk the talk" mistake, 48–50
    "separation of business and values" mistake, 54
    "top management sets the values" mistake, 50–51
    "values are soft and fluffy" mistake, 52–53
    "values conflict" mistake, 53–54
    "values police" mistake, 50

mistrust, 3, 4–6
modeling behavior, 57
morale, 32, 163–164
motivation, 35, 48, 56, 69
Motley Fool, 43–44
Mullett, Carey, 126
My Starbucks Idea program, 86

narratives
    authenticity in, 33
    creating, 99–103
    founding stories, 100–101
    trend toward new, 12–15
    See also history of the organization
NASA, pre-mortems, 73
negative feedback, 60
negative thinking, 73
New Yorker, 143
New York Times, 5
Nickels for Nonprofits program, 144
Nike, 102
Nokia, 34
Nova, David, 120
Novo Nordisk, 56

O.Noir, 146
optimism, 166
organizational evolution, 103–108, 108–109
organizational goals, 142
organizational growth, 147–148
organizational history. *See* history of the organization
organizational principles, values as, 34
organizational values, 160
outside-in perspective, 70, 84
outsourcing, 80
outward introspection, 79–83

partnerships, 166
passion, 87
patterns/cycles, 98–99
paying attention, 79–80, 80–81

performance appraisals, 50
performance challenge, 44
personal aspirations, 140–141
personal goals, 142
personal growth, 147–148
personal/individual values, 34, 58
perspectives
    offering, 127
    outside-in, 70
plateaus in values, 165–166
play integration, 126
plus/delta reviews, 74
position, leading by, 61–62
postmortems, 74
power of negative thinking, 73
power structure, 35
preferences, values as, 19, 20, 26
pre-mortems, 73
presenteeism, 140
preventable failure, 77
PricewaterhouseCoopers, 132
Princess Margaret Cancer Centre, 108,
    153
principles, values as organizational, 34
problem of authenticity, 18
problem solving, 37, 58–62, 76
Procter & Gamble, 74
psychology experiments, Milgram's,
    48–49
public perception of businesses, 4–5,
    5–6
purpose, 143–144
    defining/predetermining, 24
    evolution of, 92
    identifying and changing, 57
    loss of, 142
    reinspiring, 148–153
    unchanging, 58
purposelessness, 141
pushback, 59, 60

questions
    ability to ask, 84–85
    for determining business model, 56
    for enabling introspection, 77
    for re-creating aspirations, 150–151

rational behavior, 19
rationalization, 20
realigning values, 85
reflection, 20, 32, 63, 70–71
    See also introspection
relational work, 124–131
relationships
    authority, 36
    benefits of, 133–134
    connections through, 24
    focusing on, 115
    stakeholder, 161
    values and, 25
    See also connectedness values
repeated failure, 77
respect, 23, 49
responsibility chain, 7
rethinking values, 21
retreats, 77, 96, 126, 150
reviewing values, 44
rewards, intrinsic/extrinsic, 33
RICE (respect, integrity, communica-
    tion, excellence), 4
Ride to Conquer Cancer program, 153
rituals, 102
routines/habits, 72

safety conversation example, 162
Samsung, 35
SAS, 147
scandals, 159
    conclusions drawn from, 5
    effects of, 5–6
    Enron, 4
    Teapot Dome scandal, 4–5
    Tylenol, 55–56
Schlumberger, 76
Schultz, Howard, 118, 147–148, 149–152
Scott, Susan, 71

self
  being one's whole self, 131–133
  values and idea of, 23–26
  See also introspection
self-actualization, 148
self-assessment, for authenticity (examples), 26–29
self-discovery, 69
self-knowledge, 18
self-motivation, 35
sense of "we," 118–124
"separation of business and values" mistake, 54
September 11, 2001, attacks, 97–98
shared histories, 94–95
shareholder value, 142
Sheth, Jag, 143
shoshin (beginner's mind), 69, 85
Sisodia, Raj, 143
Skype, 104
smart failure, 77
social entrepreneurs, 166
social responsibility, 167
sounding boards, 84
space training, 73
Specialized Bicycle Components, 82
stakeholders
  check-ins with, 160–161
  conversations with, 83, 108
  creating value for, 167
  engaging, 99, 121–122
  getting feedback from, 71, 152
  involvement of external, 61
  support from, 161
  tradeoffs among, 13–14
  value creation for, 12, 13
stakeholder value, 142
Starbucks, 86, 118, 147–148, 149–152
Steam Whistle Brewing, 145–146
story sharing, 103, 111, 113
struggles, acknowledging, 98
success
  acknowledging, 98

  barriers to, 69, 70
  conditions for, 75
  differentiators determining, 139–140
  facilitating, 70–71
  recasting failures as, 78
"success breeds failure" trap, 83
symbols, 102
systems checks, 163

Taj Public Service Welfare Trust, 122
Tata, Ratan, 122
Tata Group of Industries, 122
Taylor, Greg, 145–146
teamwork, 49, 129–130
Teapot Dome scandal, 4–5
technology, connectedness through, 116
Teranet, 128–130
Time Warner, 104
Tomasello, Michael, 117
Toms Shoes, 166–167
"top management sets the values" mistake, 50–51
Towers Watson Global Workforce Study, 140
traditional values, 21
training, 73
transparency, 123
trends
  macro, 80
  new narratives for business, 12–15
  values and engagement, 11–12
  See also future orientation
trust, 161
  building, 127
  in businesses and executives, 3, 4–6
  reasons for lack of, 6, 8
truths, acknowledging, 85
truth-telling, 52
Twelpforce, 82
twenty-first-century business, 6–8
Tyson, Bernard, 76

undermining values, 10

unexpected, capitalizing on the, 78

Unilever, 41–42

upcycling, 145

US Army, 74

value chain, 7

value creation, 13, 57

value-fit approach, 37–39

values (in general)
    being true to your, 17–18
    conflict about, 3–4, 19, 22–23
    conflicting, 8–9, 50, 53–54, 58
    content of, 38
    context of, 21–22, 24
    defining, 18–23
    as process (examples), 26–29
    types of, 22
    ways of thinking about, 33
    See also aspirational values; con-
       nectedness values; conversa-
       tions about values; historical
       values; introspective values;
       mistakes about values

"values are soft and fluffy" mistake,
    52–53

values-based business models, 58,
    164–166, 167

"values conflict" mistake, 53–54

Values Jam, 85

"values police" mistake, 50

values programs, 49–50

values statements, 10, 20, 39–42
    devising, 160
    discussions following, 50
    Motley Fool's, 43–44
    showing connectedness in, 115

values through conversation (VTC),
    39, 58–62, 63
    bridging the values gap with, 63

bringing historical values to life
    through, 95–108
    conversation starters, 90
    derailed values process, 163–164
    devising vision statements, 160–161
    insights gained from, 89
    reasons for undertaking, 161
    revising, 161–162
    role of aspirational values in,
       137–139, 154, 155, 160
    role of connectedness in, 114–117,
       160
    role of history in, 91–93, 160
    role of introspection in, 67–70, 160
    at Schlumberger, 76
    taking it to the next level, 164–166
    values violation problem, 162–163
    See also conversations about values

values violation problem, 162–163

vision statements, 143–144
    evolution of, 149
    market focus in, 137–139
    Unilever's, 41–42

VTC. *See* values through conversation
    (VTC)

walking the talk, 20, 37, 48–50, 56

Wall Street Journal, 5

Warby Parker, 167

Webber, Alan, 84

We Day, 88, 100

Whole Cities program, 145

Whole Foods Market, 42, 61, 74,
    142–147

Wolfe, David, 143

workforce, empowerment of, 9–12

work/life balance, 36, 132–133, 147

Yum! Brands, 120

Zappos, 102–103, 123

About the Authors

Tom Cogill

R. Edward Freeman is university professor and Olsson professor of business administration; academic director of the Business Roundtable Institute for Corporate Ethics; and an academic director of the Institute for Business in Society at the Darden School, University of Virginia. He is also adjunct professor of stakeholder management at the Copenhagen Business School in Denmark, visiting professor at Nyenrode Business University in the Netherlands, adjunct professor of management at Monash University in Australia, and visiting professor at the International Centre for Corporate Social Responsibility at Nottingham University in England. He has held honorary appointments as the Welling professor at George Washington University and the Gourlay professorship at the University of Melbourne. Prior to the Darden School, Freeman taught at the University of Minnesota and at the Wharton School at the University of Pennsylvania.

Freeman is a co-author of *Stakeholder Theory: The State of the Art* (Cambridge University Press, 2010) and of *Managing for Stakeholders: Survival, Reputation, and Success* (Yale University Press, 2007). He is the author or editor of more than 20 volumes and 100 articles in the fields of stakeholder management, business strategy, and business ethics. Freeman is perhaps best known for his award-winning book *Strategic Management: A Stakeholder Approach* (Cambridge University Press, 1984, 2010), where he traces the origins of the stakeholder idea to a number of others and suggests that businesses build their strategy around their relationships with key stakeholders. He is the editor of the Ruffin Series in Business Ethics (15 volumes, Oxford University Press). He is also a co-editor with Jeremy Moon and Mette Morsing of the Business, Value Creation, and Society Series (11 volumes, Cambridge University Press).

Freeman has a PhD in philosophy from Washington University and a BA in mathematics and philosophy from Duke University. He was recently awarded honorary doctorates in economics from Comillas Pontifical University in Madrid and the Hanken School of Economics in Helsinki, as well as an honorary doctorate in management science from Radboud University Nijmegen in the Netherlands for his work on stakeholder theory and business ethics. Throughout his career he has received a number of teaching awards from the Wharton School, the Carlson School of Management, the Darden School, the University of Virginia, the state of Virginia, and the Academy of Management. He has received Lifetime Achievement Awards from the World Resources Institute, the Aspen Institute, the Humboldt University Conference on Corporate Social Responsibility, and the Society for Business Ethics. He has worked with many executives and companies around the world.

Freeman is a lifelong student of philosophy, martial arts, and the blues. He is a co-principal in Red Goat Records, LLC, found at redgoatrecords.com.

Joncarlo Lista

Ellen R. Auster is professor of strategic management and the founding director of the Schulich Centre for Teaching Excellence at the Schulich School of Business at York University. Prior to joining Schulich, she was on the faculty at the Graduate School of Business at Columbia University and was a visiting faculty member at the Tuck School of Business at Dartmouth College in Hanover, New Hampshire. She earned her BA from Colgate University and her PhD from Cornell University.

Auster has more than 30 years of experience as an academic and a consultant specializing in strategic turnarounds, transformations, and transitions. Working with executives and managers to successfully tackle a wide spectrum of strategic change challenges in industries ranging from manufacturing and consumer goods to financial services, she creates a shared-leadership, stakeholder-inclusive, value-creating approach that enables the firm to cultivate the short- and long-term capabilities needed for continuous evolution and success.

A multiple research and teaching award winner, Auster has been honored with the prestigious global, lifetime achievement Academy of Management Distinguished Educator Award. She has also received research awards from the Academy of Management and Management Science, and she has twice been named a Kellogg–Schulich Executive MBA Professor of the Year as well as being honored with the Seymour Schulich Teaching Excellence Award and the Outstanding Educator of the Year Award at York University.

Auster has written and co-authored several other books, including *Strategic Organizational Change: Building Change Capabilities in Your Organization* (Palgrave Macmillan, 2005); *Excellence in Business Teaching: A Quick Start Guide* (McGraw-Hill, 2005); and *Stragility* (Rotman/University of Toronto, 2016). She is published widely in academic journals, including the *Academy of Management Review,* *Management Science, Sloan Management Review,* the *Journal of Business Ethics, Human Resource Management,* the *Journal of International Management,* the *International Journal of Strategic Change Management,* the *Journal of Applied Behavioral Science,* the *American Journal of Economics and Sociology, Sociological Inquiry, Advances in Strategic Management,* the *Journal of Management Education,* and *Research Policy.*

Berrett–Koehler
Publishers

Berrett-Koehler is an independent publisher dedicated to an ambitious mission: *connecting people and ideas to create a world that works for all.*

We believe that to truly create a better world, action is needed at all levels—individual, organizational, and societal. At the individual level, our publications help people align their lives with their values and with their aspirations for a better world. At the organizational level, our publications promote progressive leadership and management practices, socially responsible approaches to business, and humane and effective organizations. At the societal level, our publications advance social and economic justice, shared prosperity, sustainability, and new solutions to national and global issues.

A major theme of our publications is "Opening Up New Space." Berrett-Koehler titles challenge conventional thinking, introduce new ideas, and foster positive change. Their common quest is changing the underlying beliefs, mindsets, institutions, and structures that keep generating the same cycles of problems, no matter who our leaders are or what improvement programs we adopt.

We strive to practice what we preach—to operate our publishing company in line with the ideas in our books. At the core of our approach is stewardship, which we define as a deep sense of responsibility to administer the company for the benefit of all of our "stakeholder" groups: authors, customers, employees, investors, service providers, and the communities and environment around us.

We are grateful to the thousands of readers, authors, and other friends of the company who consider themselves to be part of the "BK Community." We hope that you, too, will join us in our mission.

A BK Business Book

This book is part of our BK Business series. BK Business titles pioneer new and progressive leadership and management practices in all types of public, private, and nonprofit organizations. They promote socially responsible approaches to business, innovative organizational change methods, and more humane and effective organizations.

Berrett–Koehler
Publishers

Connecting people and ideas
to create a world that works for all

Dear Reader,

Thank you for picking up this book and joining our worldwide community of Berrett-Koehler readers. We share ideas that bring positive change into people's lives, organizations, and society.

To welcome you, we'd like to offer you a free e-book. You can pick from among twelve of our bestselling books by entering the promotional code **BKP92E** here: http://www.bkconnection.com/welcome.

When you claim your free e-book, we'll also send you a copy of our e-news-letter, the *BK Communiqué*. Although you're free to unsubscribe, there are many benefits to sticking around. In every issue of our newsletter you'll find

- A free e-book
- Tips from famous authors
- Discounts on spotlight titles
- Hilarious insider publishing news
- A chance to win a prize for answering a riddle

Best of all, our readers tell us, "Your newsletter is the only one I actually read." So claim your gift today, and please stay in touch!

Sincerely,

Charlotte Ashlock
Steward of the BK Website

Questions? Comments? Contact me at bkcommunity@bkpub.com.

Certified

Corporation
bcorporation.net